Praise for A Simple Guide to an Organized Life

"No matter what your challenge, you are sure to find some useful solutions. A wonderful book containing a collection of valuable organizing tips."

—Dr. Steve Adubato, Author, Media Expert

"This is a wonderful guide that will help simplify any parent's life."

—Dr. Maryanne, Author, *Simply Parenting*

"A quick and easy read that offers hands-on practical organizing advice."

—Judith Kolberg, Author, Founder of the National Study Group on Chronic Disorganization

"A must for everyone who wants to simplify their life."

—Fred Bauer, Licensed Business Coach

"Patricia Diesel's guide truly demonstrates how to create order out of chaos. Pat's tailored recommendations for individual styles were right on."

—Susan Zema, MA, CEAP

A *Simple* Guide
to an
Organized Life

Patricia Diesel

Keep It Simple Now, LLC

A Simple Guide to an Organized Life

Keep It Simple Now, LLC
14 Cottage Street
Basking Ridge, NJ 07920

www.keepitsimplenow.com

ISBN 10: 0-9789303-0-4
ISBN 13: 978-0-9789303-0-1

For more information, address the publisher.

Publisher's Note:
Throughout this book you will see, where applicable, all service
mark and trademark proprietorships for all companies and products
mentioned. Any mention of a brand name product, company or
web-site should not be considered an endorsement of that product,
company or web-site. The author has no affiliation with any
manufacturer, company or web-site and is not paid to endorse any
products.
All information and advice in this book is the result of my experience
and research along the way, or are simply common sense. Tips from
copyrighted sources are listed and credited accordingly.

This book is dedicated to my daughter,
Leigha Michelle Diesel.

"Don't forget what happened to the man who suddenly got
everything he always wanted…he lived happily ever after."
—*Willy Wonka*

Acknowledgements

To James Flachsenhaar, who believed in my vision, way beyond the twinkle in my eye. Words cannot express my gratitude.

Many thanks, to Elizabeth Faulkner, for experiencing the many hours of "getting it right."

My deep appreciation, to Dr. Steve Adubato, for all the support he has shown me.

Special thanks, to Judith Kolberg, who has taught me invaluable lessons.

To Walter O'Brien, thanks for always being there.

Introduction

As a professional organizer for many years, I have enjoyed helping my clients "create order for a simpler life." A natural outcome of my work was a desire to share my insights and techniques with a wider audience. The result is this compilation of articles re-birthed.

In many articles you will notice I refer to a particular season. This does not mean or suggest that you cannot apply these tips throughout the year.

My wish is that you will find this book to be useful and enjoyable. Remember, getting organized is contagious. Spread the news and have fun!

.

Contents

GETTING STARTED

ORGANIZING YOUR BUSINESS

ORGANIZING YOUR HOME
Home Projects

ORGANIZING YOUR HOME
Household Management

ORGANIZING YOUR HOME
Rooms And Closets

ORGANIZING YOUR HOLIDAYS

ORGANIZING YOUR PAPERS

ORGANIZING YOUR STUDENT

ORGANIZING YOUR TIME

VACATION ORGANIZATION

VEHICLE DIRECTIONS

GETTING
STARTED

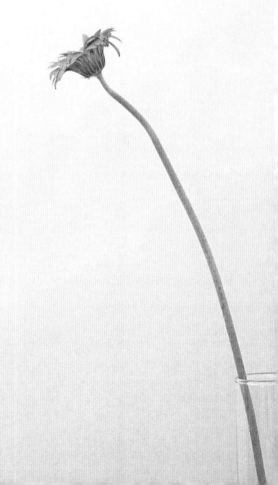

How To Get Organized

Staying organized can be difficult for many. After clearing out our spaces from time to time and making clean sweeps, the clutter seems to creep back into our homes and offices.

At the end of the day, we may feel overwhelmed because we realize we haven't caught up with all the things that still need to be done, much less begin the projects we have planned to accomplish. To make matters worse, we then begin to compare ourselves with others who we think are "more organized," which just leads us to feel even more discouraged.

Good news

There is good news. Getting organized is a learned activity. We can get organized and stay that way with proper guidance and support. The key component here is to try and understand that we are all individuals with different needs, so our approach to getting organized may be different as well.

Finding what works

It's about finding what works for you. Begin with thinking about what you need to organize so you can come up with a system that works for you, not a system that is designed for someone else.

What needs organizing?

Paperwork

- Bills and personal finances
- Mail and junk mail
- Newspapers, catalogs, magazines
- Children's schoolwork
- Medical paperwork
- Appointments, telephone calls

Household

- Closets and pantries
- Kitchen
- Living area or bedrooms
- Home office
- Garage, attic, basement

Organizing tools

Now that you have established what needs to be organized, choose a task and figure out what organizing tools you will need to help you.

- Colored file folders
- Colored pens and markers
- File rack or cabinet
- Paper shredder
- Calendar, cork board, dry erase board
- Sticky notes or flag stickers
- Clear storage bins, containers or baskets
- Label maker

Organizing rules

The key to successful follow-through in your organizing is to commit to the following rules, step by step, one at a time.

- **Dedicate 15-20 minutes to a task** – Baby steps are the key here, so you don't feel overwhelmed. Think of mini successes.
- **Keep like with like** – When sorting out your belongings, put like items together. Know the difference between your apples and oranges.
- **Everything needs a home** – Your stuff needs to be put away. Find a place where it belongs that makes sense, and then do it.

Organizing rewards

Some bonuses of an organized life are less stress, increased productivity and being better able to manage your time. But in order to get to that final reward, we may need some motivation during the process. While undertaking your organizational tasks, build in some extra incentives for yourself.

Treat yourself to a dinner or movie with a friend after completing a step or two. But most of all, pat yourself on the back for your organized behavior, you deserve it! ᵞᵞ

Know Thyself

*Conquer your organizing challenges
by learning how they came about and
which tools you need to fix them*

Do you feel there is disorganization in your life? Are you experiencing clutter and chaos in some part of your environment? Is it confusing for you when you try to choose a course of action on how to conquer your disorderliness?

The solution here is to first figure out how your state of chaos may have begun and why it is still happening.

Self-awareness

It may very well be a lack of knowledge or understanding of how to get organized, or an underdeveloped skill set that needs to be refreshed, that keeps you in a state of disorganization.

Keeping true to the theory that getting organized is a learned activity, the solution here would be to educate and support you in finding your own unique organizing style.

Also, implementing practical tools that will compliment your organizing methods can help smooth your learning process.

Temporarily de-railed?

Your disorganization could be something that was caused by a "temporary and transitional" state of affairs, which I refer to as T&T.

For example, when a significant change occurs that derails you from your normal routine, you begin to react in a coping method to help you through your transitional stage.

Such T&T occurrences can be a move or relocation of residence, a loss of a job or relationship, or even an illness or death.

Getting back on track

The key here is to recognize that the disorganization was due to unforeseen circumstances, but after the dust has settled, you work on getting back into your normal routine, pick up your organizational skills again and work on conquering whatever may have manifested in the process - piles, unpaid bills, laundry, an overload of newspapers and magazines.

Do you have CD?

But what happens if your clutter is continually occurring, if organizing has always been a challenge for you and it affects the quality of your life in some way, just about every day?

The answer could be that you are Chronically Disorganized, referred to as CD. According to Judith Kolberg, author of *Conquering Chronic Disorganization*, "Chronic disorganization is the result of the bad fit between people who organize unconventionally and the very conventional organizing methods which exist for them to use."

One of the solutions here to help overcome your CD is to figure out what type of learner you are.

Are you visual, auditory or kinesthetic? Is it easier for you to learn through seeing, hearing or moving and touching? Identifying what type of learner you are helps you choose the necessary organizing tools.

Match tools with styles

Here are some suggestions on organizing tools to help with your different learning styles. Keep in mind that it is common to be more than one type of learner. If you find that to be your case, consider selecting the tools in each category that you find to be organizing-friendly.

- **Auditory organizing tools:** audio cassettes, recorders, teleconferences, voicemail, headsets and headphones, talk to yourself, brainstorm verbally with others.

- **Visual organizing tools:** colored files, color coding, wall calendars, cork boards, dry erase boards, clear containers, sheet protectors.

- **Kinesthetic organizing tools:** clip boards, sticky notes, 3-ring binders, flip charts, pace while thinking or rock in place, walk while talking.

The Language Of Organizing

Not too long ago, while I was working with a client, she asked me to define the words "uncluttered" and "purge." Up until this point, she always thought of the two words as the same. This got me thinking. How many times has the language of organizing been misunderstood?

It's no wonder that people can feel challenged or overwhelmed when left to self instruction of an organizational task.

If you are experiencing difficulty processing a step or an instruction, while embarking on an organizational task, it very well could be that you do not understand the concept or the meaning of the word. To eliminate such puzzlement, I thought it would be a good idea to begin with some of the words used just about everyday in the organizing world.

Clutter

Clutter is a condition of disorderliness or overcrowding. To fill your environment with clutter is to make a place untidy or overfilled with objects. When we hear the word clutter, other words come to mind such as mess, confusion, untidiness and disorder.

Uncluttered

Uncluttered is not having too many objects or details and therefore not appearing messy, obstructed or cramped. Some words that come to mind are, order, neat, shipshape and organized.

Sort

Sort is to categorize or place things in categories according to shared likeness. Words that may come to mind when we hear the word sort are classify, arrange, place and separate.

Purge

Purge is to remove or get rid of something that is undesirable. We may think of words such as eliminate, remove, clear, rid and do away with.

Organize

Organize is to arrange the elements of something in a way that creates a particular structure. Words that have a familiar ring when you hear this word can be: put in order, arrange, control, fix, coordinate, systematize and manage.

Chain of command

I have too much clutter in my house. I want to have an uncluttered environment. In order to do this, I must begin to sort my stuff, purge what is unnecessary and then begin to organize.

Counting Clutter

Six factors to consider when getting organized

Understanding your organizational options amid your clutter and chaos may take some homework on your part. There are a lot more factors to consider than just going out and purchasing the right organizing tools.

1. What's your clutter about?

Are you knowledgeable and aware of what your clutter is all about? Would you consider yourself a first time offender when it comes to being disorganized or have you always felt like your surroundings have been out of control? Understanding your manifestation can be the key to unlocking the mystery to your piles, stacks and overall mess.

2. What's your comfort level?

Ask yourself some questions about your state of affairs. What's your comfort level with your environment? Is it bringing your energy level down every time you enter your home, thus leaving you feeling anxious? Or are you so used to your surroundings being this way, you just brush it off?

3. How complex is your clutter?

Does your clutter involve just parts of your home or is it in every room? Do you find you have certain habits that take on a life of their own in different rooms? Are you dropping and scattering throughout the entire house? What about your office area – organized or disorganized? What does your garage and basement look like - are you utilizing the space for its designated utility or is it your dumping ground?

4. What do you have invested?

Do you feel like there would be a greater payoff for you to become more organized in all aspects of your life? Would order provide peace and harmony and more balance for you? Do you think you would find yourself entertaining more in your home and enjoying your space?

5. How involved can you be?

What role do you want to play in getting more organized? Do you consider yourself a novice when it comes to organization or are you up for the challenge? Do you actually want to do all the work yourself, every aspect of de-cluttering or just some of it? Or would you be better off utilizing the assistance of a family member, friend or even a professional organizer, who can offer resources and education?

6. How much time do you have?

Bottom line is you want to have a clutter-free house that feels good to come home to. How much time are you willing to invest in getting your end results? Will you be making it your top priority to dedicate the time necessary or have you considered what it would be like to have someone implement an easy-to-use in-house system that would work for you? Ask yourself, how much time do I have? ☉

What's Your Clutter Saying?

*IDEAS AND TIPS TO HELP YOU LIVE AN
ORGANIZED, SIMPLER LIFE*

Do we create clutter to resolve issues in our lives, or is the clutter the issue?

When you don't want to pick up after yourself anymore, and you begin to leave things lying around your home, and just the thought of doing one more load of laundry could send you over the edge, what do you think that's really about? Yes, at times we all get tired and need a little reprieve, but setting aside the fact that we are not dealing with any major physical or mental challenge, what do you think is the underlying reason for most people's clutter?

Well I think it has a lot to do with unspoken words. The lack of communication that is between two people or a simple dialogue that needs to take place. Wouldn't you agree that whenever we begin to bottle up our feelings we start to feel an overwhelming sense of frustration and hurt? So why do we do it? What would be the worse case scenario if we did vent our feelings and state what was on our mind?

To the ordinary eye, clutter can seem like it's manifesting in ways where someone's world is out of control with stuff, but to the person who is outwardly producing the mess, they have something more important to say. It's not about their stuff, it's about the clutter that is in their head. If the mind is filled with clutter, the normal course of action would be for the clutter that's in their head to come out and pile up somewhere else.

I believe when people wake up in the middle of the night pacing the floors, making themselves a hot cup of milk, or turning on the TV, they are looking for ways to calm themselves down. Depending upon the volume of clutter that is in their head, people look for ways to soothe the chaos that echo's in the chambers of their mind.

By not being able to disclose or share their feelings out of fear of rejection, they never get the opportunity to say what is needed. The problem continues to exist and the mind stays cluttered and the outward manifestation begins its cycle again.

When a person reaches out for a Professional Organizer they are usually going through a life shift and the desire to communicate becomes stronger. They are seeking answers and solutions and want the feelings associated with their clutter to dissipate. The secret they have been harboring for a long time interferes with the quality of their life and they want their dirty little secret to be exposed. They long to be free.

If you find your living space or work environment is out of control and your clutter is interfering with the quality of your life, try the following exercise. Give yourself some time and write down your answers. Keep in mind, by being specific and detailed, the more information you can give yourself to see clearly through your clutter.

Identify the source of your clutter
What do you think is the cause of your clutter?
When did the clutter begin?

Identify your feelings about your clutter
What is bothering you about the clutter?
How does the clutter make you feel?

Identify the manifestation of your clutter
What does your clutter look like?
How are you expressing your clutter?

Identify your cluttered mind
What do you want to say about your clutter?
What would you like to tell someone about your clutter?

Identify your clutter free vision
What would your space look like without clutter?
What would your life be like without clutter?

Coaching Through The Clutter

Getting organized clears the mind and helps you focus, so you can ultimately get back on track again.

I noticed the same thing with coaching.

Just cleaning up the clutter is not enough, because it will come back. People need direction.

In the world of professional organizing, coaching is a necessary and instrumental tool to facilitate the growth process when working with people who are challenged with clutter and chronic disorganization.

Coaching can help people understand and figure out the emotions that are behind their manifestations.

But just like a coach, a professional organizer is someone who is also sensitive to their clients' needs. A professional organizer, who has the ability to be sensitive and empathetic, shows true professionalism, and this can make all the difference when it comes to supporting the client. As a society, there is this expectation that every aspect of your life must be highly organized, neat and sanitized at all times. Few people live up to that lofty expectation and as a result, feel guilt and shame.

So many people really don't understand why they are disorganized and become very upset and hard on themselves.

This is where part of the shame and guilt comes in because they think, "Why can't I get organized?" or "Organization is supposed to be easy, so why can't I do it?"

Coaching helps the client accept who they are and look for ways to overcome some obstacles and manage the rest.

It's about balance and also knowing "thyself." Professional organizing offers solutions by taking control of their surroundings, time and paper, and implementing systems for life.

When a person is tired of clutter and wants the chaos to stop, they can look for solutions and support. Whether the choice is professional organizing, coaching or a combination of both, one thing is for sure: The process of getting organized becomes contagious.

Organization not only becomes obvious in the surrounding environment, but also within the person. This, in itself, becomes a huge motivational factor for change. ♡

4 & Goal

The first and sometimes hardest step to goal making is selecting a goal. Ask yourself, "What do I really want? How can I make myself happier? If I had one wish, what would it be?"

Brainstorm and try to come up with several ideas. Then select your goal. Try to remember to keep the process simple and fun.

Put it in writing

Think of your goal as a well laid out plan, a blueprint for success. Now, put that plan into writing. By doing so, you are making a commitment with yourself and more likely to follow through.

Take baby steps

Did you know that when we undertake any type of project, if we start off slowly with a baby step or two, we will create a mini success for ourselves?

Consider applying this theory to your goal setting. For example, if you want a more organized home or environment, take small steps, room-by-room perhaps, toward your goal, to keep it more manageable and attainable.

Be accountable

Give your goal time limits. Break down your goal into three parts, short-term, mid-term, and long-term. Enforce deadlines and time constraints within each term and then measure your success. By doing so, you're holding yourself accountable, and more likely to achieve success.

Get support

If getting organized is one of your goals and you are feeling overwhelmed or not quite sure where to begin, consider getting support. Ask a friend, family member or a professional organizer for advice. With some extra encouragement, you're likely to feel less stress and be quickly on the right path toward your goal.

Tip

When expectations are too high or if we make goals to please others, more often than not, our attempts will fail. By setting realistic goals you are more likely to achieve them and celebrate your success.

Notes To Stay Organized

ORGANIZING YOUR BUSINESS

A Cluttered Desk Is A Sign Of Genius?

Turning busy into accomplished

According to The National Association of Professional Organizers (NAPO), one hour a week is spent on finding documents and 23 percent of adults say they pay their bills late because they lose them. So, I guess what I am confused about is how one may believe in the concept that clutter is a sign of brilliance.

Did you know that Benjamin Franklin once remarked, "If you want something done, ask a busy person?" I am assuming that his definition of busy meant highly competent and organized, because from my point of view, some of the busiest people I know are not necessarily the best ones to ask to get something done.

A lot of people may look busy, but does that mean they are accomplishing their tasks at hand? Sometimes, we are just plain busy looking for things that we can't find among our piles of clutter. And then we get even busier, when we have to make a list of the things we need, because we can't locate them and then have to go shopping to purchase the items we simply cannot find. Sound familiar to you?

So please help me out here - where's the brilliance again?

I know many high-functioning people who can operate under "organized clutter," but I haven't met a person yet who functions well among chaos. So let's take a look at what I mean by "organized clutter." For example, a person may have piles of note cards stacked neatly on one part of their desk in a method of chronological, alphabetical or simply colored order. In another area of their work space you may find sticky notes, lined up symmetrically on a cork board, or file folders stacked up, jutting out ever so slightly for easy recognition.

In this particular example, the person is usually operating in "pending mode." Everything is out in front of them so they can locate it immediately without the fear of losing or forgetting what is important and what action needs to be taken. It is a common occurrence for people to operate in "pending mode" when they find themselves multi-tasking, juggling a series of projects, and are constantly on the go.

However, it is necessary to point out that this person is also operating in a "temporary and transitional" mode, (where action is constantly occurring), and their method of organization of their stuff is seen as temporary housing. Their information or data has never reached its final destination, which is the permanent home for the completed task. Usually under these circumstances when the person has completed the work, the information usually goes into another pile somewhere on the floor, on top of a cabinet, but it does not stay within sight of the pending work area.

So the question is - what's your method of organization?

Do you even have one? And with the example that was before you, imagine how a person would be able to perform if they truly had systems in place and homes for their stuff.

We all know that a clutter-free environment raises your energy level and a room full of stuff zaps our very being. If a cluttered desk is a sign of genius, just imagine what an organized desk represents.

Doing A Job On Clutter

Do we have clutter in the office due to poor systems or are we simply outgrowing our space?

It is very common to face clutter challenges when your business experiences growth spurts. There can be an overwhelming amount of paper that flows through an office, leaving you with correspondence to address and then file away. Looking at your scattered papers and piles can zap your energy and leave you feeling exhausted.

And then the question comes, "Do I need a bigger office?" The answer to this is, sometimes yes, but not necessarily.

In some situations it really is about outgrowing your work space and reassessing your environment, but in some cases it's not about that.

Clutter can be a result of many things, including change. For example, a person who is used to working with an assistant and now finds themselves alone, faces not only system challenges, but time management issues as well.

Another reason your clutter can build up could be that your systems that you now have in place are no longer working for you. They need to be improved upon to align with the level of work that is coming into your office.

If you find your office space is out of control, and your clutter is accumulating to levels of insurmountable work, ask yourself the following questions:

- What organizing tools do I have?
- Do I have a hot box?
- Do I have color-coded files?
- Do I have pocket folders for my files?
- Do I have a filing rack?
- Do I have a filing cabinet?
- Do I have a cork board?
- Do I have a calendar?
- Do I have a date book?
- Do I have a phone book?
- Do I have a dry erase board in my office?

If you answered yes to any of the above items, now ask yourself if you are using the tools properly. For example:

- Is my cork board labeled or is everything just thrown up there?
- Are my files scattered all over the desk top or are they in a rack?
- Are my current or pending files in a hot box so I can locate them quickly?

- Am I using color-coded files to distinguish my different projects or items?
- Is my phone book system up to date or am I looking for contact information over and over?
- Is my filing cabinet organized and cleaned out, or do I spend too much time looking for my files?
- Am I missing appointments because I forget or does my date book or calendar remind me?

Use your answers as a barometer to see how well your current systems are working for you.

Keep in mind, utilizing organizational tools that you may not be familiar with, can act as a support system for your challenges and may just be the ticket to seeing clearly through your clutter.

Make Getting Organized Your Business

Did you know that the lack of organization directly impacts profits of a business?

If only people would spend more time investing in good organizational habits, they would experience a lot less consequences that disorganization brings, such as stress, overwhelming feelings, and financial duress.

When you are organized you are more likely to succeed in building a stronger business, because you are able to concentrate on what's important. Your vision and focus is clear, and you don't need to waste time and energy looking for items or trying to remember things because you lack systems.

Sometimes, the process of getting organized requires a new way of looking at things. By taking a fresh approach to the possibilities of what organizing can do for you, you open the door to finding new solutions to your business challenges.

To see if you are serious about making some changes, ask yourself the following questions:

- How important is the success of my business to me?
- Is my business becoming what I want it to be?
- When I look back on my business, will it matter?

By asking yourself the following questions, you can find out what areas of your business can be improved upon through organization:

- Is my business losing time and money?
- Are my business finances as organized as I would like them to be?
- Is my office filled with clutter?
- Do I have clear established boundaries?
- Do I have systems in place that work?

1. The first step to understanding how organization can play a defining factor in the growth and success of your business is to know the Golden Rules of Organizing:

- Never underestimate the power of organizing
- Creating order is essential for maintaining a well-balanced life and business.

2. The second step is listening to other people's testimonials on how organizing improved the quality of their business.

Valerie Waterman of SMD Group said the following:

"Knowing now that I am a visual learner, I realize that having visual organizing tools customized for me, really works – specifically, the color folders, the cork board and, more importantly the 30-month calendar and project/dry erase board.

Since I work out of my home office, I really found the philosophy of 'keeping the office strictly business,' changed the way I viewed things.

It helped me understand the business function it served and how structure was something that was missing from my daily routine. Viewing my office this way helps me stay focused and on track.

I didn't have the skills to be able to come up with a good system for myself, because I was too close to it. Reaching out to a professional was one of the best things I ever did for myself." ☎

Put It In Writing

Simple, but effective, thank-you notes made easy

When was the last time you handwrote a thank-you note?

Whether you are looking to grow your business or just brighten someone's day, a thank-you note can be very powerful.

What's behind the power of a handwritten thank-you note?

To begin with, personal thank-you notes are rare these days. People just don't invest in the time to send them. But when you do, you can almost guarantee that you will make the person feel appreciated and put a smile on his or her face.

In return, the recipient will remember you and when people remember you, they are more inclined to either give you repeat business, a referral or simply a kind deed in return.

A writing exercise

To prepare for the following exercise, go to a peaceful place that will be conducive to writing - somewhere that will provide inspiration and allow you to be centered.

Now, take a few moments to envision the person to whom you are writing the thank-you note. Think back to the experience that you shared with this person and replay it in your mind. Does it bring a smile to your face? Good, then you're ready to focus on the writing aspects.

How to write

In Donna Smallin's newsletter *Organized Greetings*, she suggests writing from your heart. Feel the experience that transpired which created the memory for you. Now think about what your motivation is behind this thank-you note. What is your hope for this person or client?

Write without expectations, but be honest with what your motivation is for writing the thank you. If you are looking for new business, Donna suggests, don't push. Simply express your appreciation for the experience you shared or the opportunity that was provided to you.

If a kind deed was provided from a family, friend or loved one, then your thank-you note is a token of your appreciation so communicate those words to them. Let them know how it made you feel as well.

Take a moment and think about how your thank-you note will be received. Chances are, you not only will feel more connected to this person, but they will feel more connected to you.

And remember, smile. ♡

Notes To Stay Organized

Notes To Stay Organized

ORGANIZING YOUR HOME

Home Projects

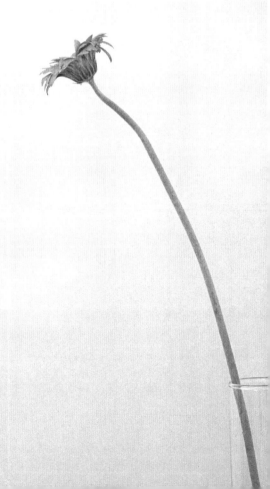

Simple Solutions

So often I hear from clients, "I wish I could get a makeover for my home," and my response is always, "What's stopping you?"

We tend to think of the big picture first before we actually lay out what our needs are. Sometimes it's the small items that really make a difference in a room, and the positioning of each item. With a few accessories, a room can have a completely new look and feel to it, and it doesn't have to cost a lot of money. It can be as simple as a new coat of paint, a swatch of fabric or reupholstering a piece of furniture.

An ordinary chair

Do you have a favorite chair in the house? What purpose is your chair serving in the home right now? Does anyone ever sit on it or does it just collect things? Do you walk by it several times a day and say to yourself, "One day, when I get around to fixing that, it's going to look really pretty?" Well, what are you waiting for?

Make it a point right now to look at that chair in a different way. How would it look if you stripped it down to the original finish and oiled it to a deep fine luster? Or, maybe, painting it with a color you never thought about before would actually add a little pizzazz. Is the seating on your chair all wood, cane or cushioned? Does it need to be reupholstered, or can you select a piece of fabric that you might have around the home to do the trick? Sometimes, an old drape or tablecloth that's been hanging around can serve as your new inspiration for a piece of fabric.

A simple shade

Lampshades seem like such a mundane item for a pick-me-up, but I have seen it work wonders in a room. Any home-decorating store has a collection of shades to choose from to give your room a new light to it, but if you are really in love with your shades and just want to accessorize them, you can do that too. By purchasing a few beads, fabric strips, some glue and a colored marker, you can make a dramatic difference.

Wall to wall

Choose a different color for each wall to complement the rest of the décor. What about adding a chair rail and painting it a different color? Or add a chair rail and pant the upper and lower portions of the wall different colors. Wallpapering one wall, or half a wall, is an option as well.

Unique headboards

A nice way to accomplish a sophisticated update to a bedroom is to update your headboard. Do you prefer wood, iron or upholstery? Here's a few cool ideas -- use other prop items for a headboard, such as a folding screen or a door, or paint a scenic décor directly on the wall.

Knob appeal

Have a piece of furniture such as a buffet, dresser or nightstand that you would like to perk up? Consider replacing the drawer pulls with glass, ceramic, stainless steel or whatever strikes your fancy to resurrect your outdated piece. Then whatever knob you select, try accenting the top of your furniture with a vase that will complement your new accessory.

One more tip

You can easily spruce up an upholstered chair or sofa by draping a colorful throw blanket over it and adding a few pillows. It's a great way to hide a stain too! ⚱

Quick Tips For Rejuvenating Your Home

The fall season is soon approaching, and it's time to begin some of those household projects. Before the weather gets too cold, you may want to consider giving your house a quick pick-me-up.

Make a list for yourself in order of priority. Remember, mini successes are achieved by taking baby steps, so think of it as one project at a time.

To help you get started, here are some tips and ideas to help spruce-up your household environment.

Outside

- Consider sealing your driveway for extra protection against the upcoming inclement weather.
- Clean out your gutters and check to see if they are attached to your house and working properly.
- Think about replacing your mailbox for a new look or applying a fresh coat of paint.
- Buy a new set of house address numbers to sharpen things up.
- Give new life to your front door by replacing the door knocker or lockset.

- Clean your windows inside and out for a squeaky clean look.
- Replace burned out light bulbs.
- Inspect your roof for potential problems or leaks. Consider calling a professional if in doubt.
- Cover all your outside patio/deck furniture and grill.
- Clean out any window boxes or flowering pots so they are ready for next season.
- Remove any dead bushes/shrubs and clean up any weeds along the way.

Inside

- Shampoo your carpet for a fresh, clean scent.
- Think about replacing light switches for a new look.
- Give your cabinets a pick-me-up by replacing the hardware.
- Change your filters in your furnace, dryer, and stove exhaust fan.
- Combat your clutter. Try choosing one drawer, cabinet or closet to reorganize one day at a time.
- Spread a little greenery. Purchase some household plants conducive to your indoor lighting.
- Install extra shelving units in your garage or basement to store any outdoor items that need to be organized.
- Check your shower head. Does the filter need to be cleaned or simply replaced?
- Consider a fresh coat of paint in your most lived in area. Pick a color that makes you feel good.

- Try replacing your old picture frames as well as updating family pictures. ⬚

Make "Friends" With Your Garage

And make room for your car

Did you know that 50 percent of homeowners rate the garage as the most disorganized place in the house, according to the National Association of Professional Organizers?

Has it been years since you parked your car in the garage? Is your garage filled with clutter, old paint cans, broken chairs, stuff you cannot even begin to recognize?

Let's take you through a step by step process to make your garage functional and organized.

Finding friends

Go through the garage and figure out what you would like to keep, donate or discard.

It's not uncommon that people tend to use their garage as a storage area for their "stuff" they can't seem to part with. If this is the case, begin by sorting it all through and asking the question; is this a friend, acquaintance or a stranger? This technique is an emotional game developed by Judith Kolberg, author of *Conquering Chronic Disorganization*.

This means, a friend you would like to keep around. An acquaintance you may need to revisit and then come to the conclusion that you can either keep, donate, or discard it. And the stranger is something you have no longer a use for. You can simply toss it and feel good about the decision.

Are you alike?

So, now you have done all the preliminary work of weeding through and de-cluttering. The remains are your friends and acquaintances left to be organized. Remember, rule number one, keep like with like. Keep all your items that belong together in one place and get ready to give them a home.

Hangin' out

You are ready to actually implement some organizational tools. Consider installing a piece of peg board on one of your walls. With a few straight hooks, you can either hang some of your tools directly, or can utilize a wire basket to house some other items.

Hanging some adjustable shelving will also give you more storage. Consider using clear storage bins and labeling them for additional clarity.

If you happen to have open studs in your garage, bungee cords stretched between the studs can create more storage by keeping larger articles tucked neatly in. Or consider installing larger hooks to hang bulkier items such as garden hoses or shovels.

Another nice tool I like is a simple paint brush rack. By hanging the brushes bristle-end down, it allows your paint brushes to dry properly and minimize the amount of dust they collect.

Here is the best part of all, if you have done a good job, you can again fit your car in the garage.

Creature Comforts

5 steps for organizing your outdoor living space

Are you dreaming of enjoying warm sunshine days and sweet breezes in the evening with an outdoor living space?

Who says you need a large budget to fulfill your dreams? With a little creativity on your part, you can transform your deck, porch or patio into a place of relaxation and enjoy the best of what both worlds have to offer - indoor comforts in the outside world.

Take stock

Begin by measuring the area you would like to transform so you can see what size space you have.

Have a feeling

Think about the overall feel you are trying to capture with your new space. Ask yourself, How do I want to feel when I am out here? Will I use this space mostly for myself and family, or will I be entertaining? Do I want a relaxing causal look, something upscale and sophisticated, or do I want to go for the funky and fun?

Complement the colors

What color do you want to bring into your new space? Go to a local remodeling store and pick up a color chart to see what complements your surroundings. Get swatches of materials and find out what works for you. Are bold stripes your look, or do flowers and solids appeal to you more? Do you want lots of color or a more natural tone?

Select furniture

When selecting furniture, there are many options to choose from but it still needs to be functional and practical. For instance, your outdoor furnishings should be weatherproof if they are going to be exposed all the time to the elements. If you prefer woods, find something like teak or other hardwoods that will hold up to the weather.

When it comes to your cushions and pillows, find something durable that will easily rinse clean and sustain the outdoor conditions. Just keep in the back of your mind; weather, moisture and stain resistant when shopping.

Dress it up

Dressing up your space with accessories can really make the overall difference for your new surroundings. A simple floor covering, such as a Dhurrie rug which is durable and washable can make quite a statement. Maybe that space in the corner would benefit from a free-standing or hanging hammock? Arranging a few potted plants or hanging baskets of flowers always adds a nice touch. For the evening, displaying votive candles, hurricane lamps or solar lighting can add a little ambience and give you a dramatic look. ☼

Planting Seeds For A Clutter-Free Spring

As we find ourselves in this glorious spring season, I am curious if this month will live up to its reputation: April Showers Bring May Flowers.

One thing I know for sure is that spring brings out the desire to become better organized.

We want to get everything in order, clean out the closets, run a garage sale and declutter the best we can.

But what is this inner desire all about? Why does spring create a yearning to tidy up and get things in place?

Is it because we know summer is coming and we want to make sure everything is caught up so we can play and have fun? Or are we just tired from the winter months of being cooped up inside with all our stuff?

No matter what our reasoning may be, the best way to approach that need to become better organized is to just do what comes naturally. Think about what is on your "to do" list. Set aside some time to conquer those items or projects. Remember to break things down into baby steps. Come up with a plan, and then go into action. This will keep your motivation from burning out too soon. Here are a few ideas to get your organization underway.

What's hanging around?

If your closet is bursting from winter wardrobe blues, why not reassess your attire by figuring out what you are really going to wear again next season.

Be honest with yourself. Have you put on any of those items hanging in your closet? Better yet, have you put them on and then realized you don't like the way you look in them? If this is the case, it's time to donate them to a friend, family member or a favorite charity. Otherwise, you will just box them up, take up precious storage space, and unpack them next season all over again.

If part of you still wants to hold on to your stuff, you can always play the friend, stranger, acquaintance game, developed by Judith Kolberg, *Conquering Chronic Disorganization*. Friends you love, so you hold onto them. Strangers you dislike, so you discard them. Acquaintances are acceptable now and then, so you either donate to a charity or give away to someone.

Cash for clutter

Are you using your garage to park your vehicle or to house belongings? If you would like to see that space converted back to its original purpose, think about having a garage sale.

You may be surprised by the big ticket items you have laying around that can bring in excess revenue.

Begin by taking one of your possessions and think about the many ways someone else would be able to use it. Then, with that thought in mind, set a realistic value for it and mark it with a little price tag or sticker. Take out at least ten more items and repeat the same process.

Now, look at what potential income you already could have generated. What better way to clean out the clutter, knowing you will be financially rewarded! If you find yourself unsure of what you can part with and are tempted to hold on to those belongings, solicit the advice of a neighbor or friend. As a matter of fact, asking your neighbor might get them motivated to join your tag sale and split the advertising costs. 🌿

How To Spring To Life
In Your Yard

Taking advantage of the extra hours of daylight may make it easier for you to accomplish some outside chores. You don't always have to choose one of your weekend days to get your tasks done. Take a little time each day and soon you will find your to-do list is well under way, and you can begin enjoying the outdoor life.

Windows

Washing windows inside and out will allow for the sun to shine in for a sun-filled happy environment. When it's sunny, the windows become very warm, allowing the window cleaner to dry too fast. Try doing this on a day that is not hot and sunny, or at the end of the day to help eliminate streaks. Don't forget to clean the window sills and screens as well.

Lawn/yard maintenance

For those of you who love to get your hands dirty, begin by picking up those left over branches that are scattered about your lawn. Start raking up old leaves and debris, allowing for early greening of your lawn. If needed, wait until your lawn has been cut several times before spreading fertilizer.

Tip: If you have an outside firepit, break down some of those branches for kindling wood.

Gutter check

Taking the time to clean out your gutters will prevent backups and overflows when heavy spring showers occur. Using a ladder and a garbage bag, simply go along the perimeter of your house to empty out any leaves or debris from your gutters and downspouts. Don't forget to wear your garden gloves.

Mildew build up

Take a good look at your exterior siding, porch, deck and steps. If you find a buildup of mildew and grime, get yourself a bucket, scrub brush and warm water with bleach or ammonia and start scrubbing away. If you find it is out of control or in areas out of reach, hiring a professional who does power-washing may be in your best interest.

Falling Into An Organized Life

Along with the clean, crisp air and the wonderful foliage the fall season provides, we tend to equate the cooler season with getting organized. We want everything neat and tidy and in its place. We would like to see the items on our to-do list be a chore of the past.

The fact that the kids are heading back to school, and we will fall into our routines again, may have something to do with these feelings.

Whatever the reason, it's a good opportunity to use our motivation and begin undertaking some of the projects we have been putting off.

Did you know?

In a National Association of Professional Organizers survey that was conducted in 2004, 90 percent of Americans planned on organizing some part of their lives, and more than 50 percent of adults say they have purchased or would be willing to purchase containers, storage systems, shelving or similar products to help them get organized.

Choose wisely

When thinking about your projects, choose a task that you can begin and end in a limited amount of time. Don't fool yourself into thinking it will take just a few hours, when in reality it may be a full day's worth of work or more. Sometimes when we "dive" right in, we bite off more than we can chew and we are left feeling overwhelmed.

Start the process slowly. This way you can begin to experience mini successes, which will leave you with a sense of accomplishment.

Ask the questions

Here are some basic rules of organizing. When sorting, ask yourself these questions.

- Do I need this any longer?
- What are the benefits of me keeping this?
- How long have I had this?
- Will I ever use it again?
- Can someone else use this?

This will help you with the process of what you can release and what you want to keep. As you begin to organize your stuff, remember to keep "like with like" items together.

Have fun

No matter what task or project you wish to embark on, I wish you the best of success. Remember, organizing can be fun. Think about making it a family day where everyone can participate. Getting organized is a learned activity, which means all ages can learn and be included. Have a great fall season! 🖋

Notes To Stay Organized

ORGANIZING YOUR HOME

Household Management

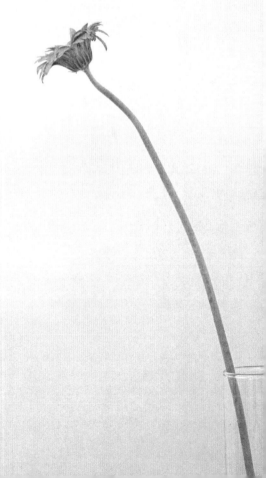

Organizing Your Family Household

One of the biggest challenges for families is finding ways to organize their schedules among one another and how to keep track of what everyone is doing. By having some simple visual aids, your family can keep abreast of everyone's activities, deadlines and appointments.

Designate an area

Select an area within your home that would make a convenient organizational station. Think about designating an area that has enough counter space for telephone access, answering machine, and if you have one, a computer. Have a caddy that will house your pens and pencils, note pads and phone book. Use a separate basket or bin for your incoming mail.

Finding the right tools

The size of your family and the amount of activities you're involved in will determine which type of tools suit your needs. Let's begin with choosing a calendar. Consider selecting, either a wall calendar, (preferably a three-month one) with spaces large enough to write in, or maybe a simple calendar that hangs on your refrigerator. The point is that you want it in easy viewing.

Another useful tool for keeping track of your schedule is a wall planner that you can easily write on and wipe off. You can purchase these completely blank or sometimes they have a separate planning area where you can write in your events. Establish what chores and tasks are being assigned to whom, and then assign a different color marker to each person.

A great way to eliminate some of the paper clutter and keep your family on target is by using a simple cork board. Begin by making specific headings using a label maker to organize your thoughts. It's a convenient way to keep important items in sight and help you remember important dates. Some of the headings may be: upcoming events, grocery list, things to do, phone messages or chore list.

Working together

To eliminate some of the stress from your hectic schedules, consider having a chore list to get your household tasks completed. Try alternating your routine by switching tasks among each other. Completing some tasks the night before can be helpful in reducing those hectic mornings. Try making your lunch and packing your backpack and briefcase at night. Or setting the table for breakfast and prepare your coffee maker. Watch the weather and select your wardrobe for a few minutes head start.

Household Management

4 MONEY-SAVING Exercises

So you made a budget. Now what?

So often the question poses itself when working with clients, "do budgets really work?"

For some, a budget is relatively easy and staying within their financial means is a breeze, but for others who know what it's like to come up short every month, it becomes a scary prospect.

Breathe easy – the following tips will help you stay on course whether you are a seasoned planner or novice budgeter.

Put brakes on impulsiveness

Next time you find the urge to pull over to a fast food place, whether it's for coffee, snacks or a quick bite to eat, think about if you really need to do this or is this simply a habit you created for yourself. The easiest way to spoil your budget is by spending needlessly on these small ticket items. Add this all up after several months' purchases, and you will be astonished on how much you spend. *Tip: Keep little purchases to a minimum.*

Think quality

Is it time for you to go shopping for yourself, or your family? When looking to purchase clothing, think in terms of classic, timeless pieces that you can build on and accessorize with. Also, don't discount consignment shops for smart buys; you may be pleasantly surprised at what you will find.

Tip: It's all about quality over quantity.

Factor in allowances

When creating your budget, don't forget to include essential purchases that you know are part of your everyday living expenses, such as holiday gifts, special occasions and recreational activities. Being realistic about your lifestyle will help keep things in perspective and won't make your budget seem so restricted.

Tip: Remember personal spending for the extras.

Cash or credit

Choosing cash over credit to make your purchases can be a difficult choice for some. There are a lot of factors to consider here, especially when it comes to your level of comfort and financial security. Some options to consider for yourself may be to think about using your credit card only for emergencies or vacation plans, or allocating a certain amount of cash each week for your spending, similar to giving yourself an allowance.

Tip: To keep a handle on your spending, always keep a record of your expenses. ◉

Update The Outdated

Save money by getting organized

What happens when the very tools you use to get organized, such as your cell phone, Internet connection and banking services need updating themselves? It may seem like you're spending money you don't want to, but sometimes updating to newer technology actually saves you money in the long run, not to mention time. Here is a list of items that may be worth looking into:

Technology

Cell Phone: Is your plan matching your current needs, or do you need more or less minutes? Does your phone provide all the latest functions that would make your life a lot less complicated?

Phone/Cable/Internet: What about your basic landline telephone service and Internet connection? Do you pay separately for these services, or do you have package deals for your cable, phone and Internet? Some of the offers that are available can save you a bundle and provide fast and easy access.

Electronic Toll Collection: Still paying cash as you go through the tolls? This is usable for most toll roads, bridges and tunnels. Signing up for one of these electronic devices can save you from sitting in idle traffic, as well as lowering your fuel consumption.

Banking

On-line Banking: Did you sign up for online bill payment or are you still manually paying your bills? Most banks offer this as a free service. Postage is up to 39 cents; consider your choices here - time and savings.

Over-draft Protection: It happens. There will be times when things get overlooked or your finances simply are a little low. For a small fee, most banks provide this service. Think of it as having an insurance plan against your checks bouncing.

ATM Withdraws – Try to factor in the amount of cash you need each week to limit the amount of your ATM stops. Most banks offer free withdraws as long as you stay under a minimum per month and you are banking with them. But remember, when visiting other banks, you will be charged a transaction fee anywhere from $1.50 to $3.

Credit Cards

Annual Fees: Some credit cards charge an annual membership fee varying from $35 to $100. By taking a look at what you actually spend on your credit card, what percentage rate you are paying and what rewards you are being offered, you can begin to figure out if it makes sense for you to be participating in this plan.

Minimum Payments: The average interest rate for credit cards is 13 percent. Do you know what your rate is? If you have multiple credit card balances and want to start paying off some of your debt, pay off the higher credit-card rate first. Remember, if you skip a payment or are even late, it can result in late fees of up to $35 or more. ❈

Smart Grocery Shopping

Be prepared

Ahead of time, before you venture off to the supermarket, clean out your refrigerator. Begin by looking for anything that you know will spoil within the next few days if not cooked or used with your meals. Anything that looks questionable, toss it, as well as any items with expired dates.

Save time

Having a grocery list reduces the number of times you find yourself running out the door for last minute items. Develop a grocery list that makes sense for you. Here are several ways to create your list:

Smart lists

- Organize your list by the items you regularly purchase such as the basics (milk, bread, butter and eggs) and then leave blank lines for additional items.
- Organize your list by category, for example, dairy, frozen foods, produce and snack foods - leaving blank lines to fill in the details.
- Organize by aisle number of your favorite food store and list all the items you purchase in that aisle accordingly.

Locate your list

Whichever list you prefer, either hand write or type it up and then make several copies. Clip together and then post it either on your refrigerator, inside a cabinet door or pantry. Staple any coupons that you will be using next time you go shopping to your list.

Helpful tips

- When running low on an item, circle it or check it off.
- Put a "C" next to items you have coupons for.
- Stock up on items such as canned goods when they are on sale.
- Take note of any items that may be spoiling due to not using it and purchase a smaller size next time.
- Don't forget to add paper items or toiletries to your list. ☕

Double Duty

Save space - and time - with new uses for everyday items

Take a look at some of the ideas listed below for multiple uses for everyday items - from taking an ordinary accessory and turning it into a fashion statement to finding natural ways to keep away those summer bugs.

Salt
- To clean leafy greens and remove the dirt and grit, swirl them around in a bowl full of salt water.
- After chopping onions, rub hands with salt and a splash of vinegar to reduce smell.
- Red wine spills – cover the area with salt and then rinse out with hot water.
    —(Sources in this section: *Real Simple Solutions*)

Vinegar
- To remove stickers, such as price tags that have gummy backings and for removing gum on clothing, apply and then let sit for 5 minutes before rubbing off.
- Get rid of buildup in the coffee pot, use one part vinegar to three parts water and run through the cycle.
- To eliminate pet and smoke odor, fill a glass of vinegar and place in an inconspicuous area.

Lemon

- Squeeze directly on hands to remove that fishy smell when handling seafood.
- Sprinkle on fruit to prevent browning – also tastes great.
- To clean and whiten cutting surfaces – plastic or wooden – rub a slice of lemon all over and then rinse.
- Squeeze in hair for a highlighter for natural blondes and then sit in the sun.

Vanilla

- Natural insect repellent, but must be clear real vanilla. It's great for mosquitoes and ticks.

Fabric-softener sheets

- To keep your linens, blankets or even clothes smelling fresh, slip a fresh sheet in between your belongings.
- For static cling, pat yourself down to get rid of the electricity.
- To use as a mosquito repellent, wipe yourself down from head to toe.

Baby oil

- On hot days when the asphalt and tar gets stuck to the back of your feet, apply baby oil to get it off.

Marigolds

- These flowers give off a smell that bugs do not like. Marigolds can be a mosquito repellent, as well as a natural insecticide if planted in the garden.

Scarf

- Choose any color ribbon you prefer, run through belt loops of slacks or skirt and tie in a bow. Also works great with neutral color clothing as a great pick me upper.
- Take a colorful scarf and tie around your purse handles for a summer refreshed look. (Sources in this section: *Real Simple Solutions*) ✂

Sweet Deals

That old saying, "You attract more bees with honey than you do with vinegar," still rings true.

How many times have you written a "to do" list, handed it off to your significant other, hoping everything would get done, and ended up disappointed when nothing was completed.

What is the difference between getting your honey to accomplish all the things on the list with a smile rather than dragging their feet and grunting all the way?

I asked several couples for their secrets. Next time you would like your partner to do something for you, try some of these suggestions to turn your ordinary list into a sweet honey of a deal.

1. When making out your list, think in terms of what is really important and not so important for you to get completed. Prioritize your list into things that can get done. This list can then evolve into easy-to accomplish day jobs.

2. When preparing your list, sometimes a smaller list needs to be formed just for items that need to serve as a reminder for your partner. On this list you may

want to include any supplies that you may need ahead of time, ranging from items that need to be purchased to just making sure anything that you already have is working properly.

3. After making your list, review it and divvy up some of the responsibilities. Maybe you can run some errands and work on some of the smaller tasks beforehand to pitch in.

4. Don't forget to acknowledge and reward your partner's efforts. Celebrate by cooking a favorite meal or doing a kind deed in return that you know will be appreciated. 🍴

The Picture Of Organization

Picture this

Your scattered photographs are now beautifully arranged and displayed in photo albums, memory books and boxes. You have them cataloged by year and organized by categories, such as holidays, birthdays, and vacations. You can locate them at any given time to share with your friends and family.

Does this sound too good to be true? Not anymore. Let's take a look at how we can begin to simplify this process and create order out of your precious snapshots.

Simple solutions

Begin by going through all your photos and separating them into important segments of your life, such as a wedding, purchase of a home, college graduation or birth of a baby.

If you don't feel like going any further, temporarily store them in something readily available such as shoe boxes or paper bags and label them accordingly. At least for now you have a home for them and have completed a portion of the process.

When you are ready, go into each box and further sort them into stages or chronological order, so each pile is smaller and more detailed. It is then you are ready to start transferring them into your choice of photo albums, memory boxes or scrap books.

Reduce your photo clutter

- To reduce the amount of photo clutter, decline the offer of a second set of prints. Take the free film instead.
- If you are not impressed with the quality of some of your developed pictures and they are not fit to be in your album, discard them.
- Scan existing pictures onto your computer and discard the originals.

A snapshot on digital photography

Essentially the same process needs to be thought through as you start downloading photographs onto your computer. Try having your developer email your photos or put them on a disk. Consider investigating different websites that offer free on-line photo albums.

Trash The Excuses
For A Clean House

Is not having a clean house becoming a crisis for you? Has your household state become chaotic and out of control? Are you beginning to make excuses for not having people over? Play dates for your children becoming a thing of the past?

Sometimes, not being able to clean or maintain your home really is about not having the time. We are so busy with our hectic lives that scheduling time to do the housekeeping is not on our priority list. So, it gets neglected until it builds up and becomes out of control.

But guess what? Your household chores also can build up simply because you do not like to do them. Therefore, we neglect them, postpone them, delay them and then they become unmanageable.

What do we want?

So, what is it that we really want? We would like to have a clean home. Studies have shown that when in a clean environment, our energy level goes up, and we become happier and more motivated. Why not consider delegating this chore to a professional housekeeper or cleaning service?

What should you look for?

Look for a good fit for your circumstances. When investigating these services, here are some questions to ask a house-cleaning company to help prioritize your needs: Are they bonded and insured? Are they owner operated or supervised? How many people will be in your home? Is it the same crew each time or does the staff change? Do you supply the cleaning supplies or do they? Do they offer weekly, bi-weekly or monthly services? Will they just clean the kitchen and bathrooms?

Clean conscience

The benefits of hiring someone to clean your home can be rewarding. You may find that the time you now have to spend with your family was well worth the amount of money spent.

You may find you feel much more relaxed and less stressed. You may even find the gift of time was given back to you to do what you like, such as catching up on those projects, enjoying some hobbies and visiting with family and friends.

But most of all you will have what you want -- a clean home. 🏠

Notes To Stay Organized

Notes To Stay Organized

ORGANIZING YOUR HOME

Rooms and Closets

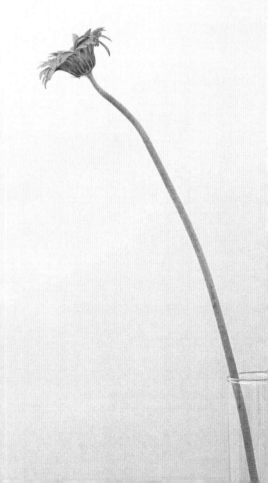

5 Tips For Sorting Your Stuff

Are your belongings piling up? No need to worry, you still can combat your clutter with these simple steps.

Begin by sorting

Choose a room in which to start that will not be overwhelming for you. Take belongings out of your closets and dressers and categorize everything into three different piles using the "friend, stranger, acquaintance, game." (Source: Judith Kolberg)

Friends you will want to keep, strangers you will discard, and acquaintances you will either donate to a charity or give away to a friend or family member.

Make a separate pile, "Unsure," for items you are undecided about.

Do you like it?

Take a good look at the items that you are unsure of and ask yourself a few questions: Do I like this? Do I love this? Will I ever wear this?

For more difficult items, put the clothes on and look at yourself in front of your favorite mirror, preferably full length and ask yourself: Would I wear this to work? Would

I wear this out on a date? And if I did, how will I feel? By the time you are done, you should have three piles left.

Organize your excess
With the items you decided to either donate or give away, you now need to determine where they are going.

Break down your piles and set up a basket labeled with a tag for each charity or family member or friend. Utilize the same process for items that you may want to hold onto for a future online sale or garage sale.

Give yourself a time limit
Sometimes, if you know you have a deadline to work with, you will stick to it. Give yourself a time span under which to work and commit to it. If too much time has passed and you still haven't released your unwanted items, the best solution here is to just bring them to the closest charity and be done with it.

Follow through
Once you get the feel for this exercise, work your way through the house, room by room. To help maintain and reduce the excess clutter throughout the year, consider doing the same steps every spring and fall as part of your clean up.

Taming Mudroom Madness

Let's concentrate on a room that usually goes unnoticed and ignored and certainly could use a spring pick-me-up - the mudroom. With just a few handy items, we can make this area versatile, useful and pleasing to the eye.

Boot rack/tray
Ideal for keeping dirty footwear out of clean closets and reducing damage to your floor. These trays come in an assortment of styles and shapes to fit your décor.

Coat rack/hooks
Installing metal hooks or wooden pegs conquers piles, backpacks or articles of clothing and keeps things neat and tidy. If you don't want to put holes in your wall and have enough room, consider a coat rack.

Shelving unit
Try to find shelves deep enough to allow for baskets or bins to be placed on them to store accessories such as purses, scarves, hats and dog leashes.

Bench/chair
No more handprints on walls from trying to balance as you remove your shoes. Finding room for a bench or chair offers a resting area to take your shoes or boots off and on.

A nice opportunity to use something fun, but still provide comfort.

Plants/flowers

Transform this once humdrum area into your own little sanctuary. Try bringing a little bit of garden indoors. Plants and flowers are a great way to add color and fragrance naturally to any room. ❁

Simple Steps To Clutter-Free Closets

During a 2004 survey by *Document Magazine,* 90 percent of Americans planned on organizing some part of their lives, of which 81 percent of the participants planned to spring clean and 74 percent planned to spring clean because they were tired of clutter.

Start with your wardrobe

When seeking a place to begin your clutter-free environment, many people start looking at their wardrobe. It's a smart idea, because this happens to be an area where we find most of our belongings for which we no longer have use. We can start eliminating the unnecessary clutter by sorting out what we really don't need or want anymore.

Unload those clothes

Did you know that we wear 20 percent of the clothes we own and 80 percent of the time the rest hangs there? (Source: *Calgary Herald* – Alberta, Canada – 1-18-04 – Karen Gram)

This is evidence that your wardrobe is probably outdated and could use some sprucing up!

- First, take each article of clothing that is hanging in your closet and ask yourself, "Do I like this? When is the last time I wore this? Will I ever wear this again?"

- Next, if you answered yes to any of the above questions, it's a good idea that you make sure the articles of clothing fit you. Try them on in front of your favorite mirror. Be conscious of how you feel in your garments. If you feel good, it's a good indication that you will look good too.

- Last, you can discard your clothes to your favorite charity, consignment shop or family or friend. With items that you choose to keep, keep like with like. Put all your dresses together and hang them in one part of the closet. Do the same with your pants, shirts and suits. Follow this procedure with anything else that makes sense for your articles and accessories. You may choose to color coordinate your handbags, shoes and belts, as well as breaking down you wardrobe by season. ⌒

Throw In The Towel

Tired of reaching for bed linens and having them tumbling down on top of you? Frustrated because you can't locate matching towels and washcloths? How about being embarrassed when guests arrive because your towels are frayed and worn?

It's time to get organized

Begin by sorting through your linens and towels. If they are worn or frayed, consider recycling them into rags for household, pet or vehicle use.

Next, dedicate shelves for specific purposes:

Bed linens

Store by color and size – king, queen, full, and twin. Store them on a shelf that is easily accessible for you to prevent them from falling. Consider purchasing closet dividers to keep them neat and orderly.

Towels

Store towels by size and color, laying the hand towel and wash cloth on top of bath towel. No more embarrassing moments here when you have sets of towels ready for yourself and for guests.

Blankets

Place blankets on the highest shelf. To make the most of your blanket space, try rolling the blankets up after you are halfway through folding them. If you find you have extra cavity space from the floor area to your first shelf, try placing blankets in a storage box or container.

A nice touch

To keep linens smelling fresh and clean, place your favorite sachet scent on one of the shelves or tuck a few fabric softener sheets between blankets. ⊨

Managing Your Meds

Let's talk about cleaning out and organizing your medicine cabinets. For some reason this area often is overlooked when we think about the items that need to be on our spring cleaning lists. By taking inventory of this cabinet, we probably will find a lot of our medications and vitamins have expired and are of no use any longer, thus giving us more storage space.

Here are some ways to begin sorting and organizing this very important and versatile cabinet:

- Begin by removing everything from your medicine cabinet and placing on a surface that's clear of clutter.

- Wipe down your shelves so they are clean and stain free.

- Start disposing of all old and expired items – prescription and non-prescription items. Don't overlook any items that you haven't used or have any intentions of ever using again.

- Now group like with like. Put all the prescriptions together, vitamins together, first-aid items, nail polishes and cosmetics.

- Organize these items on the shelves by storing the frequently used items in the front area of the cabinet. Be sure to keep all the labels facing outward for easy viewing.

Did you know?

- Medicines or vitamins should never be thrown away where children or pets may find them. To be safe, throw all of your disposals into a bag, tie it up and put it into a lidded or sealed trash can outside of the house and out of reach.

- Replacing your toothbrush every three months helps maintain good oral hygiene. Once the bristles of the toothbrush begin to splay, it will no longer be as effective in cleaning your teeth.

Notes To Stay Organized

www.keepitsimplenow.com

Notes To Stay Organized

ORGANIZING YOUR HOLIDAYS

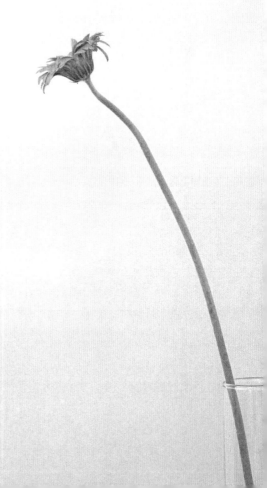

Quick Gifts

*Check out these resources for finding
the perfect Valentine's Day gift*

Valentine's Day - the day we celebrate our love of romance.
We deliver special tokens and sometimes showers of gifts
to our partners, all in the name of love.

However, sometimes we may find it difficult to find that
perfect present or we just may leave the task to find the
right thing to the last moment.

Why not replace your confusion about what to do or buy
or where to go, by checking out these online resources for
a quick Valentine's Day present.

Flowers
Roses, bouquets, flower gifts and baskets
www.flowers.com
www.myflowers.com

Gift baskets
Gourmet foods, specialty items, unique gifts
www.giftbaskets.com
www.delightfuldeliveries.com

Chocolate

Candies, jelly beans, sweets
www.candy.com
www.favoritecandy.com

Clothing

Pajamas, boxers, lingerie, slippers
www.pajamagram.com
www.lingerie.com

Beauty

Perfumes, colognes, beauty gifts
www.fragrancenet.com
www.perfumes.com

Jewelry

Necklaces, rings, pendants, earrings
www.ice.com
www.diamonds.com

Stuffed animals

Teddy bears, balloons
www.vermontteddybear.com
www.stuffedanimals.com

Personalized gifts

Keepsakes, mementos, frames
www.personalizationmall.com

Cards, love notes

www.greetingcards.com

Visit www.valentine.com and www.valentinesday.com for additional ideas. ♡

The Trick To Organizing Treats

It's that time of year again, when all the little ghosts and goblins come looking for special goodies.

With enthusiasm, our little friends will shout well-rehearsed lines of "trick or treat" countless times. You will never notice their weariness from traveling about all evening.

Are you ready for your special guests? Are you hesitant to purchase too much or too little? Are you concerned about inclement weather or not sure if you will even be home that evening? Here is a guideline that will help you out.

How much candy

Take into account how many children are in your neighborhood. Depending upon this, consider that each candy bag usually holds about 24 pieces of candy. You can safely estimate that one bag will cover approximately 24 children at one piece per child. Also, you may want to factor in that your neighborhood children will invite their friends along, so consider doubling your amount accordingly.

Another consideration is if you are going to be left with extra candy, think about purchasing the type of treat you would prefer to have in your household, so it doesn't go to waste. If at the end of the evening you see you are left with too much candy, double up on the treats you give away.

Inclement weather

Of course, the weather has a lot to do with how many visitors you will be receiving, but one never knows. Sometimes those goblins like to surprise you. First, keep their safety in mind. Make sure your pathway and steps are clear and free of any debris, especially those leaves that can become wet and slippery causing accidents. Be sure to keep your lights on so they can see their way clearly to your door.

Home or not

Sometimes we are taking our own little goblins around to trick or treat and no one is left at home to greet your visitors. Or maybe you will be out that evening, but would like to oblige your guests. You have a couple of choices. You can simply leave a sign stating that you are out trick or treating and will be home soon, or think about leaving a basket with a little note saying, "As not to disappoint anyone, please take one treat per person."

Post treats

When the kids come home with all their goodies, carefully go through their treats. Anything that looks suspicious, toss out immediately. Divide up the remaining treats into healthy and manageable amounts for your children. If you feel there is an excess of treats that you would like to share, consider having your children bring some in to their teachers or bring some in to your co-workers.

10 Ways To *De-Stress* Before the Holidays

The holidays are right around the corner, with Thanksgiving clearly in sight. It can be a very exciting time that is spent with family and friends for gatherings and celebrations. But sometimes in the midst of all this, we get caught up in the preparation and start to feel overwhelmed and stressed.

Why not consider some stress reducers to help combat any pre-holiday jitters. Pampering yourself is good for the mind, body and soul and can help calm your nerves. Engaging in some of these options can help melt away your stress and offer a nice break from your everyday life without breaking your piggy bank.

1. Take a 2 hour break and go get a manicure and pedicure.

2. Make yourself a hot cup of tea and curl up with that good book.

3. Make a date night with your partner.

4. Book yourself a date for a facial and massage.

5. Add some bubbles to your bath and just relax.

6. Try 15 minutes of meditation to get balanced.

7. Play a game of golf, tennis or your favorite sport.

8. Pick a favorite video, get your popcorn and enjoy it with the kids.

9. Take the dog for a long walk.

10. Catch up on your rest, take a nap.

Traditions To Be Thankful For

Thanksgiving is such a special time of year. This holiday is an opportunity for most to celebrate with loved ones they haven't seen in awhile. It happens to be one of the busiest travel times of the year, as the kids come home from college, family members who live far away find methods of transportation to be home, and friends gather.

For years, I have been hosting this celebration, and every year I enjoy it more. With anticipation, I look forward to my guests arriving and having them compliment my home and my cooking. As they enter, I always can count on them to say "It smells so good in here" or "Is that pumpkin pie I smell?" and, of course, "The table looks so beautiful."

But more importantly, what I yearn for is the connection and the bonding time I have with my family. It is a holiday that we take time to be thankful for all the gifts and treasures we have in our lives that we sometimes take for granted.

So, on this special holiday, I would like to say thank you for your continued support and feedback. I truly feel blessed to be able to communicate with you through my writing. Have a wonderful Thanksgiving.

Creating traditions

One of the things that I enjoy most about this time is the holiday tradition that I share with my family. Each year, we take turns going around the table as we hold hands and let each other know what we are thankful for. It is a time where we not only offer our prayers of thanks to God, but also to one another.

A fun tradition my family looks forward to is the recipe I provide for them. Each year, I try a new side dish or dessert, and I type up the recipe and leave it out on the table as part of the decoration. It is always a great conversation piece.

Thankful gifts

Why not take plenty of pictures around your holiday table this year. Select the ones you like the most and consider getting them framed and giving them out as holiday gifts to your loved ones. ♡

Surviving The Festive Season

The four weeks after Thanksgiving are usually some of the most hectic, yet exciting weeks of the year. Party planning, gift shopping and meal preparation hardly leave time to get your usual chores done and even less time for yourself. Even with the best-laid plans, we are sure to experience a wrinkle here or there.

Remember, no need to stress out, the secret to overcoming these bumps is to "keep it simple."

Let us start with the biggest culprit of all: cooking.

Smart, simple cooking
Stock Up.
Purchase as much of what you can ahead of time. Why wait for the holiday madness and risk having what you need be out of stock? Another point is that prices tend to go up for items that are popular around this season.

Buy it already made.
Maybe this holiday season, it would serve you better to buy a turkey or ham that already has been prepared. This way, all you have to worry about is making the complimentary side dishes.

Divvy up responsibilities.

When it comes to side dishes and desserts, ask your guests to help out and bring one of each. Whatever is left over, you can split together.

No time to bake?

Why not think about a shortcut with ready-to-bake cookie dough. You can still have fun with the kids by decorating them with your favorite toppings such as chocolate chips, nuts, crunched candy or whatever you prefer.

Tip: When things begin to get really busy, we tend to neglect our healthy eating habits. Set aside a time where you can prepare several meals at once such as stew, casseroles and soups. Now, all you have to do is reheat and you're ready to eat.

Give The Gift of Simplicity

Smart solutions for holiday shopping

Finding the perfect gift for everyone on your holiday list can be a difficult task. The key to keeping your spirits bright and your sanity intact is to make your holiday shopping as simple as possible. Here are some smart solutions to assist you.

Smart and simple

Eliminate the guess work

Take the guessing out of what to buy. Ask the people you are buying for to supply you with a wish list. Let them know your budget and ask them to put three items on it. You can't go wrong here.

Think gift certificates

When in doubt or have last-minute shopping, gift certificates always are well received. Be creative by thinking of what the person really enjoys or needs the most.

Some ideas for gift certificates may be a favorite restaurant, mall, specialty shop, sport, music or dance lessons, concert or play. Practical gift certificates can be for cleaning services, educational classes or even professional organizing.

Share family treasures

Do you have a family heirloom that you would like to pass down to your children or grandchildren? Whether big or small, why not wrap it up and give as a holiday gift? What a great way to start a holiday tradition.

Shop at home

Take advantage of shopping in your own home. If you're looking for convenience and do not want to fight the crowds, this is a nice solution. Sit yourself down and go online or flip through those catalogs. Just be sure to do this well in advance in case you have to return any items before the holidays.

Look for sales

Most stores offer savings anywhere from 20- to 35-percent off. And if you are a regular customer of theirs, you usually can get additional discounts as well. Why wait for the prices to go up for the holidays, go now.

Tip: While shopping for those bargains, some places may not accept credit cards. It is always wise to keep some extra spending money on hand. Just be sure to keep it in a safe place. 👜

Stress-Free Celebrations

Whether you are hosting a party or attending many celebrations, it is not unusual to start feeling a little overwhelmed.

It's a time where people tend to go all out and expectations are high. Being prepared can help keep stress to a minimum so you can enjoy yourself.

Here are some tips to follow.

Holiday Party Planning

- **Do you need extra help?** If you are seeking outside entertainment or catering services, book at least a month in advance. Make sure you have your baby sitter lined up and any transportation for the sitter or the kids, if needed. If you are hosting a party and want the house to be clean, schedule the cleaning for the day prior to the event rather than the day of. You have enough to do that day.

- **Think about your space.** Do you know what your house looks like with rooms filled with people? If you expect a large crowd, you may want to rearrange your furniture to accommodate your guests. If necessary, removing some of your furniture may not be a bad idea. Seek some help from a friend to temporarily store your belongings.

- **Choose your wardrobe.** Knowing what you are going to wear takes a lot of undue stress off you. If you will be wearing something you already have, try it on and make sure you like the way it fits. Look to see if it needs any repairs or dry cleaning beforehand. If purchasing a new outfit, do not wait until the last minute. Give yourself enough time so there is a better selection of clothes available, as well as any last minute alterations it may require.

- **Stock up on your host and hostess gifts.** Count how many parties you will be attending and then add two more to the list for last-minute invites. Give yourself a budget of what you would like to spend and stick to it, counting in the gift-wrapping costs as well.

Tip: It's always a good idea to check up on your guest list. Even though people have good intentions and RSVP with a yes, there are always the "no shows." Knowing how many guests you will be hosting, can help with your last-minute preparation. ✂

Creating Holiday "Magic"

With the anticipation of the holidays, there is so much excitement in the air. And creating a festive home brings the kid out in all of us. Try these simple and helpful tips and watch the magic happen.

Advent calendar

The countdown to Christmas morning is always a lot of fun with an Advent calendar. Children can begin each day with a candy treat, a special note or even an ornament.

Personalized ornaments

Break out the construction paper in colors of red, green, purple and gold. Have your crayons, markers, glue and glitter ready. Your inspired children will be sure to devise some creative ornaments they will be so proud of. Get some string or ribbon and they're ready to hang.

Create a centerpiece

When trimming your tree, grab some extra branches and set aside. Take the kids for a walk and gather pine cones and holly. Let the kids pick out some fun, festive balls and ribbon and their favorite scented candle. Go to your table and arrange your gatherings together. Presto, you have yourself a holiday centerpiece that will certainly be a conversation piece.

Gingerbread

Gather your family and friends around for this one. Check out www.gingerbreadhouses.com for a variety of gingerbread house ideas and other edible goodies. Get a few gumdrops, and you're in business.

Slumber party

Why not invite over the cousins and friends for a holiday sleepover to remember. Ask them to bring their sleeping bag and wear their favorite pajamas. Serve hot cocoa with marshmallows and gingerbread cookies. Read classic holiday tales or turn on a holiday video while the kids snuggle up. To make it extra special, why not ask Santa to make a guest appearance. Talk about holiday memories!

Hosting Holiday House Guests

Here are a few tips to keep you calm and ensure comfort for guests who are visiting overnight for the holidays.

Be prepared

Do your guests have any special needs that you may not be aware of? Are food allergies a concern? If so, ask ahead of time. So you do not disappoint your guests or, better yet, don't have to run out at the last minute, ask what they prefer to drink or eat. Chances are they will like what you do, so there will be minimal fuss, but you want to be sure.

A word about pets

Pet lovers sometimes take for granted that other people are too. But there are times when people may be uncomfortable around our little friends, or they could simply be allergic to animals. Consider keeping pets in a separate area of your home. Clean and vacuum thoroughly, especially the bedroom they will be staying in, to minimize any reactions to their hair or dander.

The little things

So many times when we travel, we forget to pack something, such as a toothbrush or comb. Be the host who is truly prepared and have trial-size toiletries available for your guests. Place these with the towel set you select for them and leave in their bedroom. This will truly be appreciated and make them feel at home.

Keep them involved

Maintaining your family routine while having guests can sometimes be a challenge, so why not ask them to participate in family activities? Chances are they will feel like part of the family and may even have some fun. You never know, they may even have a suggestion or two.

Essentials

To provide extra comfort for your guests, sometimes having a few extra essentials can guarantee a comfortable stay. Review the following list and add any items that you think will be needed: alarm clock, bathrobe, books and magazines, closet or luggage rack, pitcher for water and drinking glasses, and toiletries. And if you want to have a little fun, try leaving a mint or candy on their pillows at night. (Source: Jeff Davidson, *The Joy of Simple Living*.)

Notes To Stay Organized

ORGANIZING
YOUR PAPERS

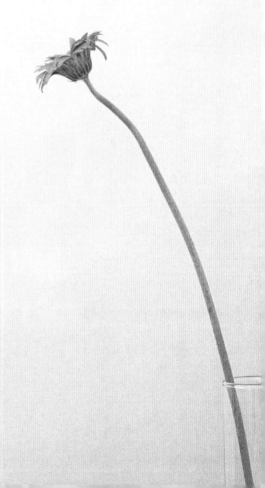

Paper Trail

A step-by-step guide to managing paper

Combating the daily amount of paper we handle can be daunting and frustrating, to say the least. The tremendous amount of paper we receive each day usually does the two-step shuffle, over and over again. Before we know it, we find heaps of paper scattered about our countertops, desks, window sills or any place we manage to drop them. Here are some tips to help you manage your excess paper flow:

Gather supplies
File folders, hanging folders, labels, markers, garbage bags, file rack, file box or cabinet.

Pick a starting point
Choose a place that is the most bothersome to you that you would like to see clutter free immediately.

Identify
Pick up the papers one by one and ask yourself, "What is this? Do I need to keep this? Can I throw it out?"

Sort

"Action" or "Urgent" papers I think of as a hot file that needs immediate attention. I suggest a red folder that will stand out for you and label it with whatever word will grab your attention.

Bills to "pay," put them in a folder labeled "Bills to Pay." I associate this with finances, so I recommend a green folder, for the thought of money.

Papers that need to be "read or reviewed," label them, "To Read." I relate this to the color yellow, which is soothing and calming.

"School work," or papers that represent education, I suggest the color blue that signifies anything academic. Label accordingly.

Discard

Anything that is considered to be junk mail, or not of use to you, throw it out or shred it.

Give it a home

Any folders that you feel need to be in sight because they require action, put them in a file rack and leave them on your countertop or an area that you will be able to respond to. Any remainder files, file away in your file cabinet or box.

Begin again

Use the above steps to start the process over on the next pile of papers. Be aware of your energy level. If you feel tired, pick and choose another time or day to begin. Before you know it, your surfaces one by one will become clutter free.

How To Stop Junk Mail

Tips on organizing and reducing the volume of unwanted mail

Did you know that paper use is growing six to eight percent each year? The number of pages printed between 1995 and 2005 more than doubled (Source: Xplor International). The excess amount of paper that is accumulated from junk mail can be overwhelming and leave you feeling frustrated with the amount of time it takes to sort through it all.

Here are some tips and solutions to help manage and reduce your overflow and put an end to it once and for all.

Time
Dedicate 10-15 minutes each day to sort through your mail. If you're not very mindful of time, try using a watch or a timer to keep yourself on track.

Distinguish
Decide what is junk mail versus personal or bills. Make separate piles for each category. Don't be concerned right now about opening the mail, just get it sorted.

Dispose

Make a commitment to toss out your junk mail immediately. Standing by a garbage can while opening your mail will make this obligation easier for you. If you know it's junk mail, don't bother opening it. Throw it out right away. This will save you not only time, but eliminate unwanted paper and piles.

Stop

One way to stop your junk mail is to write your name and address on a postcard or letter and send it to:

Direct Mail Association, Mail Preference Service, P.O. Box 9008, Farmingdale, NY 11735-9008.

It will usually take several months before you start to see a reduction in your flow of junk mail. ✉

Taking Inventory Of Personal Documents

So often we put our most important papers, financial, legal and other significant documents, to the way-side with the intention of someday putting them into their proper places. This is a must for your "To Do List!"

Being able to locate and identify family documents is very helpful if you ever find yourself in an emergency situation. It can save a lot of time and prevent undue stress for you and family members.

To get you started on the right track, consider breaking down the following categories in color-coded folders and then dedicating a file drawer just for these items. Then make a master list identifying all of your documents for easy access. For fast identity, put color bullet marks next to each item on your master list so it corresponds with your file folders.

If you feel uncomfortable about having these documents in your home, consider renting a safe deposit box at your bank.

Blue

Identification papers, including birth certificates, social security cards, passports.

Red

Family documents, including marriage certificate, divorce agreement, adoption papers.

Green

Estate papers, including deeds, titles and wills.

Yellow

Personal documents, including insurance policies, registrations, home-inventory papers.

Tax Tips

Tips for organizing your tax-return documents

It's that time of year when we must start preparing for our annual tax returns. As we begin the process of getting our paperwork in order, I am sure most of you say, "next year, I will be better organized."

Since it is your responsibility to provide all the information required for preparation of a complete and accurate return, it is definitely to your advantage if you have all your records in order.

By doing so, you can help increase your chances of getting the proper deductions, credits and write-offs you deserve.

Ever-changing tax laws and paperwork burdens make the preparation of your tax returns more and more demanding and time consuming each year. Having your information in early to your tax-return provider will give them the time to offer you more personal and professional services and help reduce the chances of error.

Organize your documents:
- Write out a list of the types of statements you get on a monthly and/or quarterly basis. Think about categories

for a filing system that will help trigger your memory as you go through this process.

- Once you've determined your categories, organize them by broad subject and then by subsubject. Example: Medical is the subject, and health coverage and dental coverage are the subsubjects. Travel is the subject, and parking and tolls are the subsubjects.

- Find a permanent home for your documents such as a filing cabinet or banker's box.

- Each tax season, go through your file and pull out what you need and toss what's not needed.

Things you should know:

- Do not destroy documents, cancelled checks or other data that are the backup for the information on your taxes. They may be necessary to prove the accuracy and completeness of your return to a taxing authority under an audit or other such scrutiny.

- If your tax return is not completed by April 15, you need to file for an extension. Most providers will apply for an automatic extension for you if your paperwork is not in.

- CPA firms usually hold onto your tax returns for a period of three years. However, it is your responsibility to keep your returns permanently, along with the documentation backing them up, in a safe place.

- If the need should arise for copies of your return older than seven years, and you cannot locate your copy, they can be requested for a fee from the IRS. ⚑

Conquering Your Piles

Are you a piler?

Do you have piles and piles everywhere? When you walk into your home do you see piles on your floor? What about on your steps? Counter tops?

In your living area, do you have piles next to your sofa? When you walk into your office, are there piles all over your desk? What about behind your chair? How about on top of your filing cabinets?

What are your piles?

Are you even aware of what your piles are? Are they piles of magazines, books, catalogs? Or are they piles of unopened mail? Piles of bills never paid? What about piles of paperwork never filed away? Maybe they are piles of files that need to be reviewed?

Who are the pilers?

Did you know that 25 percent of people in the work force save things in piles instead of files? According to the National Association of Professional Organizers, the office isn't the only place they let clutter accumulate. When surveyed, 59 percent describe their house as "somewhat messy."

Why do we pile?

It has been suggested that our piles may represent unfinished business of some sort. For instance, we may begin to pile to remind ourselves to do something, such as open the mail, order something from that magazine or catalog, catch up on reading, or review the files for an upcoming project.

The problem with this is if we never go back to sort through these piles, they will continue to grow.

Since we are all individuals, our piles represent something different to each one of us. For some of us the piles are simply reminders of tasks that still need to be done, but for others, they may represent unfinished business on a much deeper level.

What to do?

If your piles are simply tasks that need to be done, why not try the 15-20 minute rule. Each day, dedicate 15-20 minutes to a pile and start paying some of those bills. Order those items that you wanted to purchase from the catalogs. Go through your magazines and only tear out the articles that you know you will follow up on. Maybe take the full 20 minutes to catch up on the reading you need for that upcoming project.

If your piles require more attention than that, consider taking maybe an hour a day to start sorting through them. Have a garbage bag and shredder by your side. Anything that can be discarded, toss it immediately. Start making yourself some action files for the papers that need immediate attention, such as bills, appointments, and phone calls. For everything else, try organizing it by category on what makes sense to you.

Don't be concerned about getting everything filed away right now. You can dedicate some time in the future to filing once your piles are conquered. ❁

Overcoming "Infomania"

Weeks, maybe months of unread magazines and newspapers are stuffed into paper bags and stand in long rows in the basement or garage. It usually starts out with the intent to read them, so the piles begin in the den, reading room or study, but time passes and not a single paper is read. So, the piles make their way to the stairwell, until eventually, the ritual of bagging them up and carrying them into their holding place begins again.

Are you a person who is challenged with a collection of reading material and don't know what to do with it? Well, first we must find out what the attraction is and what is so appealing to you.

"The allure here is a combination of things: newspapers and magazines are inexpensive, make an easy read, and are simple to acquire. The subject matters are diverse and wide ranging, which hooks the infomania," says Judith Kolberg in *Conquering Chronic Disorder*.

According to Judith, an "infomania" is a person who finds joy indulging in simultaneous, diverse interests from any and all sources.

So you see, anyone who finds themselves challenged with wanting to keep up with current affairs or has a thirst for worldly events, is going to be wildly attracted to this type of reading material right from the start. And what's even more fascinating is it's quite typical for the person to convince themselves to hold onto the newspapers and magazines, because they believe if they don't get to read the whole paper, they will at the very least get to clip and tear out the sections that they find the most interesting.

When a person starts to accumulate stuff, in this case newspapers and magazines, and it is severe enough to be classified as a true compulsion, seeking a professional mental-health expert is recommended. However, if you feel the quality of your life can be improved upon by your own motivation, and you are up for the challenge, there are some options available to you.

If you are holding onto your papers because you feel you may need some information at a later time, the first thing you can do to cut down on the consumption, is to realize that 70 percent of newspaper and magazines are advertising. If you are not going to use any of the coupons or offers, then toss these out immediately. Also, if you are worried that you threw something out and now you need it, just about all published material is accessible through the Internet, so no need to worry; you can find it.

Here are some of Judith's additional tips:

- Ask someone to clip and file your articles for you

- Join a clipping service

- Learn to skim

- Cancel subscriptions that are too much alike

- Rediscover the library

- Immediately discard newspaper sections you never read ✿

Notes To Stay Organized

Notes To Stay Organized

ORGANIZING
YOUR STUDENT

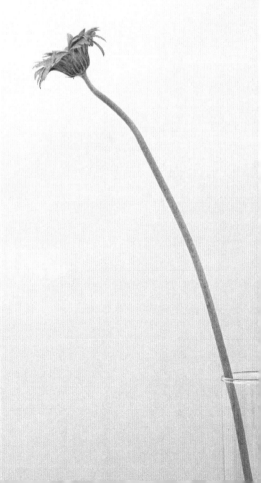

Creating Back-To-School Routines

As summer is winding down and we begin preparing for our children to go back to school, I think one of the most difficult situations we encounter is getting back into our routines.

Adjusting to structure or even finding it, after having endless summer evenings, can be very challenging to say the least.

Why have a routine?

Believe it or not, children need routines. Having organization within your household is healthy for your kids.

They may not always appreciate or like your rules, but there is something to be said for knowing what is to be expected. It makes your children feel safe and secure. But more importantly, having a routine shows your kids that you care enough to teach them how to become responsible people.

What does a routine feel like?

Having a routine and being organized reduces the level of stress within your home. Providing structure and discipline within your environment can bring you some peace of mind. Do you have a routine that is working for you now? And if not, what can you do next to incorporate one into your life? Why not start with these simple steps to begin the process?

Morning routine

Start the day off right! If you find yourself nagging and yelling down the hall to wake your children up, stop! Try going into their room and lightly whisper their name as you gently caress their hair. Maybe a little introduction of what the weather is like and how much time they have before they "go" to school is enough to get them up. Try turning on their favorite music.

After-school routine

More likely than not, kids are hungry when they come home from school. Having a usual snack time is something that kids look forward to. Try having their favorite snacks available and alternate the days you offer different ones.

Letting them watch television or play outside, allows them to unwind and rejuvenate after their day. Setting specific times for your kids to enjoy these activities helps them manage their time when it comes to their homework and chores around the house.

Bedtime routine

Having a bedtime ritual is usually the best time for kids. They enjoy knowing that after everything is said and done, they have their nighttime routine. Setting a ritual bath-time and story-time followed by lights out, ensures your children a good night's sleep. Having a good night's rest is important to your child's overall health and performance in their school and study habits.

Organizing Your Student

Study in organization
What you can learn...
from the way you learn

A believer that getting organized is a learned activity, I recently found out that so is taking a test.

Preparing for a test is about developing skills that fit your own learning style and then putting those skills to work to help you take the exam with ease.

In my opinion, this is not taught well enough to children and students. By simply knowing and understanding what type of learner you are, you can implement strategies to help alleviate your stress.

I always thought of myself as a strong visual learner, only to find that I am actually a very strong auditory learner. Because I like visual tools for organizing, I thought I should use the same strategy for test taking.

I discovered that utilizing kinesthetic and auditory tools actually will help me tremendously. Not only will it help me prepare for exams, but it will also help whenever I need to commit facts to memory.

If you find yourself struggling, or have children with similar challenges, I encourage you to figure out your strengths and weaknesses in your learning styles. Set some time aside and experiment with different tools.

Below are some methods to help develop and work with your skill set, whether you are organizing or studying.

Seeing is believing

Tools for the visual learner, someone who learns through seeing, include:

Colored hi-liters: The colors will help break down and categorize different segments that you need to compartmentalize.

Colored flag-stickers: The color stickies will help you find areas that you need to return to and break down into different thought processes.

Dry erase board: Write down the important facts and then bullet them with differently colored markers. This will help distinguish important elements you need to remember.

Have you heard?

An auditory learner is someone who learns through hearing. These tools are useful for study and for getting organized:

Audio cassette/CD: Repeating the material over and over will reinforce your memory.

Recorder: Record your material the way you need to hear it and then keep playing it over and over.

Talking: Talk to yourself or have someone else with you to act as a sounding board.

On the move

A kinesthetic learner absorbs knowledge by moving and touching. Try these tools for remembering and learning:

Sticky notes: Write down your key points and place them where you can review comfortably.

Pace: Think about your material as you walk around. Keep reciting it in your head.

Walk: Walk around while reciting your information out loud. Take however long you feel comfortable.

Rock in place: Rocking back and forth also will help clear out your head while you commit things to memory.

Low level of noise: Don't have outside distractions such as loud music or noise pollution. Find yourself a quiet place. ▭

Clean Up

4 ways to help kids learn about organization

Did you know that by having a routine and being organized you can reduce the level of stress within your home?

Providing structure and discipline within your family is a way to instill good habits for your children that not only will foster their well being, but also bring you peace of mind in the interim.

Make it routine

One way to teach your children how to become better organized is by having a routine.

Routines show children how to be responsible, thus making them feel safe and secure. A simple routine can commence with setting a ritual bath-time and story-time followed by lights out, which promotes a good night's rest and overall good health.

Make it clean

Showing your children how to clean their rooms and maintain the messiness is another way to show your children the skills of organization and reduce the risk of accidents.

Introducing the concept that a child's room is the place of retreat to de-stress from the day's worries, will help that child take pride in and teach respect for their belongings.

Make it simple

A smart way to lower your kid's level of frustration is to simplify their lives. Take a look at what activities your children are involved in and then rate the level of importance to their well being. If your children are continually stressed out, ask yourself what's the payoff? Does it make sense to continue down the same path or do some of the activities need to be cut back?

Make it last

Depending upon the age of your children, think about what you can begin teaching your children right away that will become a life-long skill for them. Is it learning how to boil water and working your way up to cooking a simple meal? How about sorting the laundry, then progressing to doing the wash and maybe even ironing? Simple household chores such as taking out the trash and vacuuming the floor, are smart ways to introduce segments of good-housekeeping rules.

Children are products of their environment and a clutter-free home promotes a clutter-free mind. 🏠

Healthy Habits

Five tips to help children eat healthfully
during the school year

When summer is at a close and school is in session, it's time to think again about making wise choices for breakfast and healthful school lunches.

In a recent study, children who regularly ate breakfast had higher standardized test scores and were better behaved than children who skipped breakfast. It's also known that energy levels decrease around late morning.

One way to avoid unhealthy eating habits for your children is to keep them involved. Allow them to be in the kitchen when preparing any type of meal, including their school lunches. Ask questions about the foods they like and talk to them about the importance of eating healthfully. This will help them develop smart food choices.

School days can be rather long and without the proper nutrition, your children can begin to feel tired and sluggish.

To help maintain a healthy outlook and keep your kids alert and ready to learn, here are some quick tips:

Make veggies fun

Cut vegetables into bite-size pieces and dip in an assortment of dressings.

Pack fruit

Pack at least one serving of fruit in their lunch – applesauce is a good substitute.

Remember the power of 3's

Strive for three whole grains, three colors in fruits and veggies and three dairy servings when planning out the daily menus.

Simple sandwiches

For sandwiches, try tuna salads or chicken salads. If you choose lunchmeats, pick low-fat, lean meats.

Refuel often

Whether you opt to have your children do their homework right after school or play outside, the first rule is to remember that your kids need to get refueled. You can recharge their batteries by serving them a quick snack of fruit, vegetables, yogurt or nuts. Providing chips or candy will only increase their appetite and make them hungrier.

While your kids are in school, you cannot control what time they are going to eat, but when they are home you can manage a routine.

Begin with the three-hour rule. Go no more than three hours between meals and snacks. Remember, kids tummies fill up fast, so you don't want to overload them.

The key is to give them energy by eating healthy, not have them feel sluggish by eating too much or waiting too long between meals.

What To Get Before Getting Your Kids Off To College

It is the month of August. My daughter will be leaving for college soon. We have approximately four weeks left to go. In our household, there are surges of excitement that hit like lightning bolts every now and then, yet there are moments of concern and worry. The excitement of knowing she is embarking on her new life, yet worry of the challenges she will face in search of her new identity.

Before they go

I wanted to experience something special with my daughter before she left. I felt it would be important for us to bond and create some lasting memories together that we could always look back on. Since the state of Maine always held such precious memories for me as a young woman, we decided to venture off to this lovely state. While exploring the beautiful coast-line, we discovered something about ourselves, as well.

We discovered that we both had tremendous respect and admiration for each other - not only in the roles that we have played up until this point, but a newfound understanding for the transition that was about to occur in both our lives.

We shared tears and many laughs, and yes my daughter who is all grown up, still wants to hug me and quietly hold my hand. At times, we talked it seemed for hours on end, yet when stillness did set in, we were comfortably content.

Whether your bonding time is going out for dinner, a quite walk in the park, or an afternoon ball game, my sincere wish for you is that you seize this opportunity to be close to your child.

Stuff you need

I hope the following list helps you identify what your specific needs are to make your transition through this amazing time somewhat calmer and simpler. Remember, each college is different as is your child. Pick and choose, add or delete from the list, but most of all, have fun with it!

Organizing/storage items

- Storage boxes/drawers/trunk
- Garment bags
- Shoe bags/rack
- Hangers
- Hamper
- Laundry basket/bag
- Duffel bag
- Over-the-door organizer

Bedding

- Comforter
- Blanket
- Pillows
- Mattress padding/cover
- Sheet sets
- Featherbed
- Backrest

Bathroom

- Towels/face cloths
- Robe
- Flip-flops
- Shower caddy/tote
- Shower mat
- Toothbrush/toothbrush holder
- Soap/soap holder
- Cosmetic organizer
- First aid kit
- Vanity mirror

Dormitory Room

- Alarm clock/radio
- Desk lamp
- Sweeper/vacuum
- Throw/area rug
- Wastebasket
- Door mirror
- Desk accessories

- Cork board
- Computer/printer
- TV/TV cart
- Telephone
- Surge protectors/extension cords
- Hooks
- Iron/ironing board
- Flashlight

Personal

- Pictures of loved ones
- Photo albums/boxes
- Wall art
- Your favorite something
- And of course, clothes, undergarments, shoes, jackets, etc. 👕

Get Shopping

Back-to-school checklist for off-campus living

For me, the month of August is bitter sweet.

It is a time of vacationing and having fun, but it also is a time of departure for my daughter.

Once again, she is college bound, and the anticipation is mounting.

Preparing our list of what is needed for dorm life – or, this year, I should say, studio apartment living -- is quite a twist from the previous year.

Due to the fact that she is now responsible for her meal preparation and cleaning of her own bathroom and living space, there should be quite a learning curve, to say the least.

My hope is that as a professional organizer and domestic diva, that I taught my daughter well, and it reflects in her new environment.

This year, her shopping list has changed quite dramatically in terms of what she needs and no longer needs for her new space.

Added to this list are items that I would categorize as desired needs, more so to express her new independence as a young woman living off campus.

As we ventured off on our shopping spree, I secretly kept my fingers crossed that this new growth spurt was not going to impact my pocket book too severely.

The good news is, by being organized and prepared with a shopping list in tow, it not only kept us focused, but it helped us remain true to our budget.

So, when my daughter went star gazing down each and every aisle, I was able to bring her back to reality, keep our purchases on target, and our overall experience cost effective.

Below is a list of what I found we needed. But remember, each child is different, as is each situation and college requirement.

Pick and choose from the below list, and have fun with it!

Clip & Carry

- ❏ Area Rug
- ❏ Bathroom Garbage Can
- ❏ Bathroom Floor Mat
- ❏ Cleaning Supplies
- ❏ Dish Towels/Oven Mittens
- ❏ Floor Lamp
- ❏ Food Wrap/Storage Bags/Containers
- ❏ Full Length Mirror
- ❏ Groceries
- ❏ Hot Plates
- ❏ Iron/Ironing Board
- ❏ Kitchen In A Box – pots and pans, silverware, plates, cups, and utensil organizer
- ❏ Kitchen Garbage Can
- ❏ Laundry Hamper
- ❏ Shower Curtain/Liner
- ❏ Tea Pot/Coffee Maker
- ❏ Vacuum/Sweeper

- ❏ Duffel Bag
- ❏ Hangers
- ❏ Shoe Rack
- ❏ Storage Boxes/Shelves

- ❏ Backrest
- ❏ Blanket
- ❏ Comforter

- ❏ Featherbed
- ❏ Mattress Padding/Cover
- ❏ Pillows
- ❏ Sheet sets

- ❏ First Aid Kit
- ❏ Hygiene Items
- ❏ Towels/Face cloths
- ❏ Robe

- ❏ Alarm Clock/Radio
- ❏ Computer/Printer
- ❏ Desk Accessories
- ❏ Desk Lamp
- ❏ Flashlight
- ❏ Hooks
- ❏ Surge Protectors/Extension Cords
- ❏ TV/TV Cart
- ❏ Telephone

- ❏ Favorite Something
- ❏ Pictures of Loved Ones
- ❏ Wall Art 🖼

Notes To Stay Organized

www.keepitsimplenow.com

Notes To Stay Organized

ORGANIZING
YOUR TIME

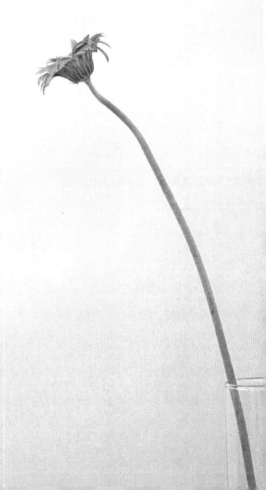

So Much To Do, So Little Time

The phrase "time management" is contemporary right now. We probably hear these words just about every day - whether it is in the office, at home, or simply echoing in the chambers of our mind. But in order for us to manage our time wisely, it would help if we first understood what time management really is.

Let's begin with the word "time." According to Webster's Dictionary, time is a system of distinguishing events. A period with limits. Now let's look at the definition of the word "management." Management is a skill in handling or using something successfully.

It would be safe to say that "time management" is about developing a skill during a limited period where an action, process or condition exists or takes place successfully.

What is this thing called time?
- I don't have enough time.
- Where did the time go?
- Do you know what time it is?
- I wish I had more time.
- It takes so much time.

Sound familiar? What are some of the things you don't have time for? What challenges are you having in managing your time? Where would you like to spend more time?

Circle of time

Draw a circle. Now divide it into 8 pie shapes, with each pie segment or slice representing the amount of your waking day that you spend on each of the following things:

- Relationships
- Career
- Housework
- Homework

- Family
- Worship
- Self-Care
- Activities

It's all about balance

Does one pie segment look way too big than all the other pie segments? Is your slice for fun way too small compared to your slice for work?

Everyone must make their own decisions as to how much of each day to allocate to each part of their life, but looking at it graphically with this pie chart might show you if your day is off balance or just about right. If you need to balance it better, trim a little time off a large slice and move it to the smaller slices. ◉

To Do Or Not To Do—
That Is The Question

Indecision

Have a lot of good ideas but can't choose one and act on it? Spending too much time weighing the pros and cons of your ideas? By being indecisive you are capable of seeing the wisdom of any side, but you are also crippled to take any course of action.

Cost factor

Your indecisiveness may also be affecting you in ways you haven't even thought of. Such as the way people may perceive you. If you are habitually slow in making decisions, people may not put a lot of trust in you and think you are incapable. Of course it works both ways. If you are a person who is too quick to make decisions, you may be viewed as inflexible and rigid.

Fears

Why do we have difficulty making decisions? What are we afraid of? Well, we could have a fear of the unknown. We may have a fear of making a mistake and looking inadequate.

The following are some tips I found in *Fastread Time Management*, by Lesley Bolton.

Tips for making decisions

- **Stay open-minded** – There are always different ways to look at things. Keep your options open when making decisions. You don't want to ponder forever, but by being open minded and looking at all the choices, you don't doubt your decisions.

- **Consider consequences** – Make note of the pros and cons of your decisions. Look at the cause and effect of each pro and con. Look at the risk factor and the odds of it happening. This will help bring the solution to a head.

- **Talk it through** – Not only writing down your thoughts but being able to clarify them by talking to someone else will give you some clarity. Having feedback from someone who is willing to listen and help goes a long way.

- **Sleep on it** – A little time away from the decision sometimes is a good thing. Rather than rushing into your decision if you're hesitant, a good night's sleep sometimes does the trick. You will wake refreshed and have a news perspective, maybe even some new ideas.

- **Now do it** – By now you're comfortable with your decision. You gathered the information required for yourself. Go for it! ☺

The Art Of Multitasking

Multitasking is the concept that seduces us into thinking that we will save time by performing two or more tasks simultaneously.

What do you believe?

Do you think by performing two or more tasks at a time you really do save time, or do you think it's a convenient way to begin too many tasks and never finish them?

Does this scenario sound familiar? You start brushing your teeth, you realize you want to put a load of laundry in, the phone rings and just about now you hear the tea pot whistling.

The next thing you know, you have a toothbrush in your hand, your arms are full of laundry, your phone is on one ear while you're making yourself a cup of tea.

Interesting, but I'm not quite sure that is what multitasking is all about.

Now what about this scenario? While stuck in traffic or waiting in the doctor's office, think about all the times you have said to yourself, "I could be doing a thousand things right now." For these situations, multitasking could really come in handy.

Next time you find yourself in one of these situations, make use of your time wisely by trying some of the following:

Waiting for an appointment

Catch up on your reading. Work on your knitting project. Sew those buttons on that blouse.

Watching TV

Sort and fold the laundry. Do some ironing. Clean. Water the plants.

While on the phone

If the conversation doesn't require in-depth listening skills, consider unpacking your groceries. Start your dinner. Wash the dishes. Unload or load the dishwasher.

Eating lunch

Open your mail. Read your email. Shop on-line.

Long commute/stuck in traffic

Catch up on the news. Listen for the weather report. Play those instructional tapes or audio books you wanted to hear.

Idle time

Write your grocery list. Cut out coupons. Plan your menu.

Organized Shopping

How does a fashion expert keep a professional organizer organized?

In my quest to find some new outfits, I realized it might benefit me to ask for the assistance of a personal shopper. I have suggested to clients with wardrobe challenges that they ask for the guidance and assistance of a fashion consultant. Maybe it was about time I took my own advice.

Not being too familiar with how the process works, I just walked right into a major department store and asked for a personal shopper.

Within minutes, I was introduced to my new best friend, and whisked away to my very own private dressing room. With plenty of room to swirl and move in my new surroundings, I was comfortable and ready to hear what she had to say.

First comes image

First, my personal shopper needed to understand the image I wanted. She educated me on the importance of dressing according to your body image. That was the first step in the selection process for finding my new attire. From an organizational point of view, I knew she was sorting through my likes and dislikes, trying to find a style that would best suit my needs.

Getting organized is a learned activity, and so is the art of fashion. Personal shoppers must be, and are, organized in their own way. They implement the steps necessary to acquire that certain look you are after. Without the proper guidance, this step can be overlooked. It makes the difference between a good outfit and dynamite attire.

Search begins

So with her new-found knowledge of me, my personal shopper began her search to find just the right garments for a perfect match. Upon her arrival, I was amazed at her choices. I was thinking abundance, but she zeroed in on quality over quantity. Colors were also an integral part of her selection process. As with any style or flavor, blending is essential to the overall picture you are trying to draw.

Simple selection

As an organizer, I thought of this as a baby step. Simply, she was not overwhelming me with stuff. She was narrowing down her selection, processing the information I gave her, and breaking it down for me.

"Excellent," I thought to myself. I immediately liked her style because I could relate to it. She was not just throwing clothes at me. She was teaching me, showing me, and educating me on the art of dressing.

Final touches

Once we narrowed down the clothes I was going to keep, the fun really began. It was accessorizing time. Wow! Now, this is where the final touches are critical to making an ordinary outfit look smashing. Like any good organizing tool, they are only as good as you use them. In fashion, your wardrobe gets better with a little extra effort to make it work completely in your favor. From shoes, to scarves, to jewelry, these extra accessories really made the difference with the final look I was trying to accomplish.

So as an organizer, what did I learn from this encounter?

I discovered it was a really smart way to shop because it allowed me to take full advantage of good time management skills. My personal shopper did all the research and work, allowing me the luxury of enjoying the experience on a whole new level. Having her assistance afforded me the opportunity to have fun, with her added insight. I felt less stressed and could ease my mind about making the right or wrong decisions.

As I walked away with my new, multi-use fashion items, I also left with a new respect for another profession. It helped me understand how organizing does play an integral role in just about every profession, even in the world of fashion.

Personal shopping definitely provided me with what I needed - an organized way to shop, with lots of perks, and the end result of looking like a million bucks on a reasonably priced budget. 👜

Making Time

*Try one of these five routines
to add time to your day*

Back to school season brings about new class schedules, after school activities and an overwhelming amount of paper. Add to the mix, shopping for clothes and school supplies, and the looming question pops back up; "When am I ever going to get organized?"

Usually people wait until things are a disaster and then they jump in and try to get organized without a plan, leaving them feeling consumed by their stuff. They get overwhelmed and give up.

In order for your plan to be successful, it's important to know what has worked for you in the past and what did not. In other words, before you go into action, know your "do's and don'ts." Begin by asking yourself some questions:

- What systems and strategies worked well for me before?
- What systems and strategies did not work well for me?
- What chores or tasks do I enjoy doing?
- What chores or tasks would I like to outsource?

- What has held me back in the past from getting organized?
- Why is it important to me to get organized now?

A key contributing factor to successful organizing is to have a routine. Routines provide structure and discipline in healthy doses. The idea is to have daily rituals put into place so they become a habit. Here are some tips from the National Study Group on Chronic Disorganization:

- Start by scheduling things on a daily basis with approximate times for completing tasks.
- Take at least fifteen minutes at the end of each day to look at the calendar for the following day.
- Get things out and ready for the following day's activities every night.

Recommended routines

1. Items needed for the next day, such as keys, purse, brief case, backpack, should be placed, ready to take, at the door where you leave. To provide additional peace of mind, try putting things in the car the night before.

2. Another component to successful organizing is using your time efficiently. The use of a timer can help you set limits for completing tasks and frame your time in a more manageable way. Choose your tasks for the day. For example, make phone calls for 30 minutes,

file papers for one hour, and work on a project for 45 minutes. Set the timer for the allotted time. When the timer goes off, move onto the next task.

3. Learn to break down large projects into smaller parts. Develop mini deadlines for completing your tasks. Remember, baby steps are the key to success. Take breaks while working on long-term projects and reward yourself for completing tasks on time.

4. A good habit to get into is doing one task at a time. For example, collect trash from all over the house at the same time, or put all the dishes in the dishwater at one time.

5. Delegate the things you don't like doing or you feel you're not good at. Example: Hire a housekeeper, a painter, a bookkeeper or a secretary. Higher success comes from the tasks we like to do. ✺

6 Steps For Shrinking Stress

We know that too much stress in our lives can create many physical symptoms for us, but what happens when the level of stress we are under causes us to become disorganized?

Studies have shown that when we lose things or forget where we put things, make silly mistakes, or start to go somewhere and then forget why, these can be symptoms that you are on overload.

If you can relate to any of the above symptoms, be gentle with yourself and begin to understand that it's time to start taking better care of yourself.

If you set some priorities and get organized, you can reduce your stress and save some time in the process.

Here are some tips that can help:

Plan your day

Get organized the night before by planning the next day. Choose what clothes you will wear, pack your lunch, take care of any loose ends that evening to free up your morning schedule.

Get enough sleep

If you find yourself doing tasks well into the late hours, consider setting the alarm as a reminder it is your bedtime. A well-rested person has a well rested mind.

Arrive early

Where ever you need to be - your job, appointment, school activities - getting there a few minutes earlier will help get you settled and more organized.

Watch your time

Wearing a watch or simply having a clock in your office will help keep you conscious of your time for proper planning. Giving yourself a little extra time can eliminate some of that worry.

Decide what's important

Simplify your life by figuring out what you do and don't want to do. Some things need to be done and some don't. Think of this even when it comes to invitations and social gatherings; select the best and leave the rest.

Use organizing tools

Implementing wall calendars, bulletin boards, message boards, and datebooks for family notices, household lists, and personal events will help facilitate the scheduling process in a more organized fashion.

Notes To Stay Organized

VACATION
ORGANIZATION

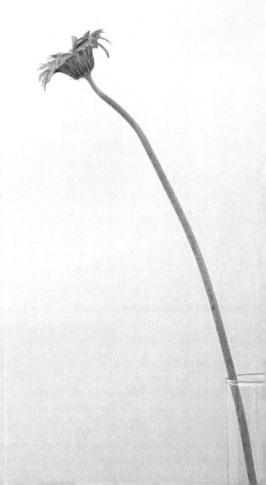

Organized Bliss

8 tips for getting the most from a day at the spa

Is there such a thing as finding refuge from the daily chaos? Is it possible to find a sliver of heaven to bring order to our daily grind?

Recently, I was given the gift of ultimate pampering - a day at the spa.

I was curious to see if by partaking in the luxuries a spa had to offer, such as steam baths, massages, and aromatherapy, would be a worthy alternative to finding peace and tranquility for my weary mind.

My ultimate day consisted of a *Cleopatra Special*, which included a milk-and-honey bath combined with a scalp massage for approximately 30 minutes. Following that, I was escorted into another room by the same person for a 60 minute Aromatherapy Massage.

Here, I was presented with different types of botanicals from lavender to mint, to increase my physical and psychological well-being. Next, it was off to my one hour Youthful Glow Facial, Lavender and Lemongrass Pedicure and final destination, Spa Manicure.

Did I find my peace?
Of course I did.

But as an organizer, I wondered how spa owners can improve upon certain services to bring about the best possible results. And upon leaving, what could they offer to sustain the essence of the client's experience once they entered their daily routine again.

I don't think it was a coincidence that while resting in the waiting room before my treatments began, I met a couple who owned their own spa in another town.

They told me how they like to frequent different spas just to keep up on the latest therapies and to see how they may improve upon their own services.

So as an organizer, what did I see differently from the ordinary eye? Keeping in mind how the couple I met were looking for ideas to keep their spa refreshed and renewed, I offer the following suggestions for those considering a visit to a spa and for those who own spas:

1. Point of entry is very important. Being greeted and escorted to your shower and locker room is essential and makes you feel welcomed. And it's a good opportunity to get questions answered.

2. Request a mini tour of the spa so you can see other services that are available for future visits.

3. Look for a preprinted list of your scheduled spa treatments and appointments. This would be helpful for planning your visit.

4. Ask about downtime between treatments. You can use this time either to catch a drink or small snack to replenish and make the complete experience more enjoyable.

5. Finding a spa that offers a food menu for lunch or dinner service, with a relaxation room in which to enjoy the meal, would be the ultimate in pampering.

6. Upon leaving the spa after your treatments, look for a suggestion card and drop-off box to share your thoughts on your visit.

7. Sending guests off with a spa bag with sample products and information on your spa would keep me thinking of returning.

8. Sending me away with some quick tips on how to maintain my well being would be beneficial. 🐚

Slowing The Pace

The kids are home from school and you have lots of idle time to spend with your family.

But why do we always think that we have to spend exorbitant amounts of money to have fun? Why do we conjure up these grandiose ideas of how our good times are supposed to be?

Considering that our children's lives today are far more hectic than ours probably were, they could benefit from some good, old fashioned fun, when times were simple and the pace was slower.

Hit the books

Begin with your local library or bookstore. Free story time and activities are offered for children of all ages, including book clubs, writer's forum, bedtime story pajama parties, and special guest appearances for pictures and autographs of your favorite characters.

Park it

Look into the parks and recreation department. For a nominal fee, your children can sign up for a variety of activities that are offered through these programs, such as archery, tennis, roller- blading, arts & crafts, and so much more.

Pack a picnic

Choose your favorite place. Maybe it's the park or the beach, or maybe the excitement of "discovering" the perfect spot by taking a ride in the car. Maybe it's just right in your own backyard. Wherever it is, pack yourself a basket, backpack or cooler with your favorite foods, snacks and drinks, including your place settings, and enjoy. Don't forget your blanket or table cloth to spread on the ground.

Rough it

Who says you have to find a campground to pitch a tent? Your destination can be your own backyard. If you don't have a tent, ask to borrow one or try making your own. All it takes is some creative thinking; blankets, sleeping bags, pillows, flashlight and some great storytelling.

Let it rain

Plan for a rainy day. Attend a matinee, go to a museum or sea aquarium. Why not take your family to your favorite restaurant or café for lunch or dinner? Go get ice-cream, catch up on some shopping, bake a cake, have a tea party, play a board game. The possibilities are endless!

Keep it simple

And don't forget these simple activities that we take for granted: bike riding, playing hop-scotch, drawing with chalk outside on the driveway or sidewalk, flying a kite, playing catch, and yes, lots of hugging.

Tips For A Relaxed Summer Vacation

As we approach summer, the season for de-stressing and leaving our worries behind, we are going to get you geared up and prepared for your vacation time. To ensure a relaxing vacation, being organized is the first step to enjoying your leisurely getaway.

Create a packing list

Creating a packing list enables us to properly prepare for those necessary items that we so often overlook. It also helps us to reduce the risk of forgetting the very important items that can have a huge impact on how our vacation begins. Think about what makes sense for you and either add or subtract from the below list.

- Cash, credit cards, traveler's checks
- Airline tickets, passport, reservation information
- Eyeglasses, sunglasses, contact lenses, cleansers
- Camera, film, video camera
- Makeup and toiletries, sunscreen
- Prescriptions, medicines, vitamins
- Jewelry, hair accessories
- Bathing suit, beach towels, beach gear
- Under garments
- Clothing
- Shoes, sandals

Gather the essentials

- Start by gathering all your important documents together: airline tickets, passport, hotel reservations, car rental confirmation and advanced tickets for events, etc.
- Next, place them in a clear, see-through pouch or holder to make them easy to identify.
- Last, put them in a place that is accessible when needed, such as handbag or front of a carry-on luggage piece.

Sensible packing

Place heaviest items on the bottom, light-weight items next and wrinkle-prone clothes on top. Don't forget to pack a plastic bag for dirty clothing.

If you know your hotel will be supplying toiletries, don't pack them.

Use a name tag, business card or a simple colored ribbon to set your luggage apart. ☆

Five Simple Steps For Safeguarding Your Home

Having peace of mind that your home is safe and sound really can make the difference between relaxing or stressing out while you are on vacation.

Try taking these extra steps to help alleviate some excess worry.

1. Mail/newspapers

Ask a neighbor, family member or friend to collect your mail while you are away. If you are uncomfortable asking someone, go to your Post Office and ask for Form 8076, "Authorization to Hold Mail."

You can even go directly on-line to www.usps.com to complete this form. Contact your newspaper delivery person or call the circulation department and ask them to suspend service for the time you are away.

2. Spot check

Erring on the side of caution, having someone check inside your home to make sure everything is OK is a smart idea.

Consider hiring a professional house sitter for this task if you do not have someone you trust.

While doing a periodical check, they can also provide other services such as bringing in your mail, watering your plants, and pet sitting if necessary.

3. Lights on/lights off

Purchasing a timer for your lights is a great way to appear that someone is home. You can purchase these at any hardware store. Alternating your radio and TV on a timer is a good idea as well.

4. Keys

Locking up your keys is the key to insuring your home's safety. Even if you are asking someone to pitch in and come over while you are away, it is best to not leave any spare keys unattended. That extra key you have outside as a precaution should be left with a neighbor during your absence.

5. Officials

Let the police know you are going to be away and ask them to do a neighborhood watch on your home. Supply them with a phone number and address of where you can be reached in case of an emergency. Also, leave other contact numbers such as a family member or close friend. 🏠

Tips For Traveling With Your Best Friends

Getting ready to travel with your pets? Not sure what to do?

Well, knowing first hand what it is like to travel with a pet that gets motion sickness, I went onto the American Animal Hospital Association (AAHA) website, www.healthypet.com, and it offered these following tips to help you and your pet have a smooth and comfortable ride together.

- Take a few short rides before the trip to help prevent nervousness or motion sickness. If this becomes a persistent problem, consult your veterinarian. Some pets may travel better while tranquilized.
- Many states require pets be restrained while moving in a vehicle. Buckling up or using a pet carrier helps eliminate them from wandering about and causing distractions.
- Don't allow your pet's head to extend outside the car window while traveling. Particles of dust and debris can penetrate the eyes, ears and nose, causing injury or infections. Excessive amounts of cold air taken into lungs can also cause illness.

- Remember to pack your pet's favorite toys, treats, food, water bowl, and leash. A first aid kit should also be carried along.
- Give your pet small portions of both food and water and plan to stop every two hours for exercise. Give your pet its main meal at the end of the day when you've reached your destination.
- Consider having your pet examined before you leave. If your pet is on medication, bring plenty of it for the trip. Prescriptions cannot be dispensed by another doctor without seeing your pet first.
- If an emergency occurs while you are on the road, you can call the American Animal Hospital Association at 800/883-6301. Be sure to travel with a copy of your pet's medical records.
- Make sure your pet is wearing I.D. tags. Carry health and rabies vaccine certificates, particularly if you will be crossing the border into Canada or Mexico.
- A follow up exam upon your return should be considered to determine if your pet picked up any diseases while away.

Tips On Preserving Vacation Memories

Did you know that Americans are averaging only about two to two and a half weeks of vacation, while Europeans take five? (Source: *Just Enough* by Laura Nash & Howard Stevenson)

Vacations are pleasure-filled experiences associated with family and friends, which uplift our spirits. Memories speak of adventure and wonder, a magical time that says, "I was there."

Considering this, here are some tips for capturing special moments to create lasting memories.

Plan ahead

Pre-addressed labels

If you are thinking about sending postcards to your family and friends, or maybe mailing that special gift for someone, bring a pre-addressed sheet of mailing labels with you. This eliminates the trouble of having to carry an address book.

Travel Rolodex™

Really jazzed up over a certain restaurant, hotel or site? Bring some extra Rolodex™ cards with you and jot it down. It's a great way to organize these places of interest that you would like to revisit or pass along to friends and family.

Journal

Sometimes the only way to capture the feeling of the moment is to write about it. Maybe for you it might mean drawing or sketching. Keeping a journal is a wonderful way to personalize your experience.

Gathering souvenirs

Souvenirs are a tie to our memories. But what do you do with them once you get home? Decide how much space you are willing to dedicate to memorabilia. If space is a challenge, keep the items that are most precious to you.

Showcase special memories

To capture vacation memories, invest in organizers designed for collectibles, such as shadow boxes or display cases. Try purchasing an oversized frame and surround a center image with some of the postcards you collected and write captions for each one.

Countless options

Seashells - Display in glass jars or vases. Make a necklace. Use as bookends.

Driftwood - If large enough, can serve as a wall plaque or even a headboard.

Flower Petals – Press and preserve in your scrapbook.

Matchbooks – Display in shadow boxes or glass jars.

Notes To Stay Organized

VEHICLE DIRECTIONS

Getting On The Road Safely

If you plan on driving a long distance for your vacation, make sure your vehicle is up for the challenge. Consider having your car professionally inspected for peace of mind. Also, be aware of any recalls on your vehicle that need to be attended to.

Did you know that there were 30.6 million recall notices in 2004 according to the National Highway Traffic Safety Administration? Following these safety measures can reduce your chances of having unfortunate mishaps along the road.

Simple steps
- Oil change – recommended every 3,000 miles
- Tire pressure and air – check the wear and tear of tires as well
- Fluid levels – anti-freeze, transmission, water, windshield fluid
- Wipers – make sure they are functioning and in good condition
- Spot check – review the entire vehicle looking for any trouble, such as broken hoses or belts
- Check the last time you had your car in for a tune-up

Before you go

Go to www.fhwa.dot.gov/trafficinfo for road conditions such as excess traffic, accidents or road construction.

Go to www.mapquest.com for directions and to get a map of your destination.

Go to www.aaa.com for help with airline reservations, hotel reservations, car reservations, maps & directions, and more.

Go to www.safercar.gov. or call 1-888-327-4236 for safety recalls. ◉

Car, Truck Or Mini-Mess?

*Tips for getting your vehicle clean
and keeping it that way*

When summer is at a close, I bet it's safe to say that like everything else, your automobile could really benefit from some organizing. After countless trips with the kids and pets, the inside of your vehicle probably could use some sprucing up. Try following these simple steps for a cleaner, refreshed auto.

Unload that mess

Take a clear bag or container with you and load it up. Bank receipts, baby bottles, cups, pens, pencils, crayons, coloring books, etc. The idea is to get everything out. You can sort through it later.

Clean and vacuum

Now take a garbage bag and dispose of all your remains that can be thrown away. If you notice any stains on your carpet, try using a spot remover and let it sit for 10 minutes before vacuuming. If you have a vacuum with a hose long enough to reach those hard to get spots, then go for it. Otherwise, if you can be quick, you can get yourself an excellent vacuum for about 75 cents at your local car wash.

Wash the exterior

Give your car a quick spin through the car wash. If you haven't had your car washed for quite sometime, consider asking the attendants to pay extra attention to the details, such as your hubcaps and moldings. You may want to think about a wax application as well.

Make a nice interior

Purchase a car freshener but only open it halfway. Sometimes the scent can be too powerful right away. Next, invest in a seat organizer. You know the kind, the one that hangs over the seat with lots of pockets. This way you can store all the items that you would like to have in your car, such as a pad, pens, flashlight, kid's books, etc.

Tip: Find out your car wash policy. Some places offer a free re-wash if it rains within 24 hours.

Car Care

Tips for keeping your vehicle 'like new'

What would it take to preserve the look of your car?

"After that new car smell has evaporated, pride of ownership usually declines," said Thomas McLaughlin, Manager of AAA Mid-Atlantic Auto Repair.

Since cars are typically more reliable than ever, the deterioration of a vehicle usually comes from neglect of caring for your car. It's not appealing to anyone to drive a dirty vehicle, yet people do it.

Did you know that emotionally we are more inclined to purchase a new car when we don't feel good about our vehicles? We like to drive something shiny and new. So our own negligence can actually be costing us money.

Let's take a look to see how you can begin to take a few simple steps to keep your present vehicle looking and smelling like new, with minimal time and effort.

Get sparkle
- To maintain that sparkle, annual waxing with quality products keeps the painted surfaces looking great. It's

your choice if you have it professionally performed or you roll up your sleeves and do it yourself.

Get energy conscious

- Take heavy items out of the trunk that are unnecessary, this will help with your gas consumption and give your vehicle an overall clean pick-me-up.

Get clean

- Remove the trash when exiting your vehicle.
- Wipe down the dashboard, console, steering column and all interior surfaces that have accumulated dust or dirt.
- Wipe door jambs and sill plates that you see whenever you open the door.
- Open the hood and remove the moisture retaining leaves that promote rust and block air from the climate-control system.
- Clean the front and back windshields on both sides with window cleaner.
- Choose an air freshener that's your favorite smell

Get under cover

- Keeping your vehicle garaged will preserve its appearance. If this is not an option, utilizing a car cover will do the trick. (Source: AAA World 2006) ✵

Notes To Stay Organized

Notes To Stay Organized

About The Author

Patricia Diesel is the founder of Keep It Simple Now, a professional organizing company that provides a "coach approach" service to individuals, entrepreneurs and corporate arenas. A columnist for the *Courier News*, she has been featured in publications such as *Cosmopolitan*, and *Garden State Woman*. She has made guest appearances on TV and radio shows, including *Good Morning America, One on One with Steve Adubato, Dr. Keith Ablow, WABC* and *WOBM*.

Ms. Diesel is a Certified Empowerment Coach, a member of the National Association of Professional Organizers (NAPO), and a Chronic Disorganization Specialist holding a Certificate of Study in Chronic Disorganization from the National Study Group on Chronic Disorganization (NSGCD).

Born and raised in New Jersey, she resides with her daughter, Leigha, her dog, Cooper and her cat, Marbles.

Seminars and Public Speaking

For more information on having the author speak to your group or organization, write to:

Keep It Simple Now, LLC
14 Cottage Street, Basking Ridge, NJ 07920
Email: Info@KeepItSimpleNow.com
(908)766-9670

Helpful Organizations

Keep It Simple Now, LLC
908-766-9670
www.keepitsimplenow.com

The National Association of Professional Organizers
847-375-4746
www.napo.net

The National Study Group on Chronic Disorganization
916-962-6227
www.nsgcd.org

International Coach Federation
859-219-3580
www.coachfederation.org